Key Stage 3

 **Oxford** I

GW00374772

Medieval realms *1066-1500*

IAN DAWSON *and* PAUL WATSON

Oxford University Press 1991

Acknowledgements

The publishers would like to thank the following for permission to reproduce photographs:

Library of Arras: p73 (bottom) (M266); Bibliothèque Nationale, Paris: p53 (bottom) (Ms Fr 599 f58), p54 (top), p58, p68; The Bodleian Library, Oxford: p13 (top) (Ms Laud Misc 636 f57v), p15 (Ms Douce 366 f89), p31 (bottom) (Ms Laud Misc 720 Pt II f226v), p46 (centre) (Ms Ch Berk 504), p52 (top right) (Bod. roll 157 no 53), p53 (top) (Ms Bod 764 f41v); The British Library Board: p24 (top), p37 (Cott Ms Claud B.II f341r), p44 (top right), p45 (top) (Add 27695 f14v), p46 (bottom left and right) (Add 42130 f163v); Courtesy of the Master and Fellows of Corpus Christi College, Cambridge: p25 (Ms 16 f215r), p30 (top) (Ms 171 f265), p55 (Ms 61 Fr), p59, p60; Courtesy of the Master and Fellows of Trinity College, Cambridge: p6 (bottom) (Ms R 17 1 f281r), (centre) (Ms R 17 1 f9r), p7 (top) (Ms R 17 1 f62v), p11 (Ms R 17 1 f2363r); E. T. Archive: p67 (Bibliothèque Nationale, Paris), p76 (top) (Musée Condé, Chantilly); Giraudon: p33 (Bibliothèque Nationale, Paris), p38 (Musée Condé, Chantilly); Sonia Halliday Photographs: p32 (bottom left), p76 (bottom); Michael Holford: p4–5, p21, p30 (bottom) (Reproduced by permission of the Provost and Fellows of Eton College), p35 (top and bottom), p39 (top left), p45 (bottom right), p70 (top), p77 (left); Mansell Collection: p43, p46 (top); Mary Evans Picture Library: p39 (top right); The Museum of London: p32 (right); National Portrait Gallery, London: p70 (bottom), p71 (top), p73 (top); Royal Commission on the Historic Monuments of England: p71 (bottom); Scala: p45 (bottom) (Galleria Nazionale, Palermo); Snark International: p65; Victoria & Albert Museum: p74, p77 (right); Weidenfeld & Nicholson Archives: p22, p24 (top), p29 (top right) (BL Harl Ch 43/British Library), p52 (bottom) (British Library, Add 39843 f6v), p54 (bottom) (British Library); Woodmansterne Picture Library: p24; Reproduced by kind permission of the Dean and Chapter of York: photographer Peter Gibson: p52 (top left) (St William Window, York Minster); ZEFA: p13 (top), p14, p29 (bottom), p32 (top left)

Cover photograph: E.T. Archive/Musée Condé, Chantilly

Illustrations: Christopher Chaisty: p40, p79; Martin Cottam: p10, p17, p23, p25, p34, p50, p57, p59, p72; Anthony Knill: p8, p13, p14, p18, p47; Fiona Powers: p3, p22, p24, p36, p42, p63, p64; Melvyn Wright: p15

Maps and diagrams: Taurus Graphics

IIII **Preface**

This book is structured as an investigation into life in the Middle Ages. It focusses on the central question: 'Was the Middle Ages a time of change?'; which can be explored and answered by pupils at a variety of levels, depending upon their ability. Having established the question, the book invites pupils to put forward an initial hypothesis, using their existing ideas, assumptions or prejudices. This hypothesis can then be developed or amended as pupils move through the material. The initial hypothesis and subsequent changes can be recorded by pupils in their own books or, if they are working in groups, as part of a wall-display. The conclusion to the book asks pupils to produce their final answer, and this will enable them to see how far they have come in their understanding of the Middle Ages.

The central question about change in the Middle Ages was not chosen haphazardly. The focus on change, continuity and causation means that pupils can develop their understanding of key elements of Attainment Target I without the need to resort to 'add-on' exercises. Opportunities for recording pupils' work in relation to these and other Attainment Targets

are provided in the exercises indicated by the headings in the chart at the back of the book. The other British core books in this series are similarly structured around ideas of change and causation; other titles in the series give pride of place to questions linked to other Attainment Targets. Details of this, marking schemes and homework sheets can be found in the accompanying Resource Pack.

The structure of the book is flexible, offering different routes through the content. The investigation can be pursued chronologically, taking the chapters in order. Alternatively, a more thematic approach would use the four Living and Working chapters as a unit, the two England at War chapters together and so on. Overall, the content in the book more than meets the content demands of the National Curriculum. It is, therefore, possible to treat some pages as extension material which may not be covered by all pupils. Additionally, chapters 3 and 7 can be taken as class projects with groups of pupils pursuing different topics and then pulling together their conclusions using the grids on pages 20 and 49. Little specific direction has been given on the use of group or individual, oral or written work so as not to infringe teachers' freedom of choice.

Ian Dawson   Paul Watson

Conquest!

Thorold wiped the sweat from his eyes and took a fresh grip on his battleaxe. Below, at the foot of the hill, the Norman knights were regrouping for another charge. Thorold had no idea how long the battle had lasted. He felt as if he had been fighting for ever. Now it would be decided quickly.

Thorold felt the ground shudder as the Norman horsemen pounded up the hill. He wasn't watching them. He was crouching under his shield, waiting till the arrow storm finished and the thunder of hooves told him that the horsemen were almost on top of the English shield wall.

Thorold and the rest of the housecarls — the elite of the English army — faced their enemy. Ignoring the Norman spears they swung their great battleaxes. Horses and men screamed as the terrible blades cut into them. The charge quickly faded. Thorold gulped for breath as he watched the Normans turn to regroup once more. Or were they ... could they be ... running away?

Away to the right and left, Thorold watched English soldiers break from their lines to chase the Normans, certain they were heading for their ships. Thorold and the other housecarls awaited King Harold's signal before joining the chase. Victory! It was victory!

Then the Normans turned. Was this part of a plan? Many Englishmen were caught in the open, unable to climb back up the slope quickly enough to reach safety. Most of the men who were now killed by Norman swords and lances had been harvesting crops in their villages only weeks before.

Once more the Norman cavalry was gathering for a charge. The English line was weaker now. Thorold again took shelter beneath his shield as the arrows hissed through the air. ...

Only minutes later all the English housecarls lay dead around their king. The Norman cavalry had finally broken the shield wall; before or after King Harold was killed nobody knows for certain. England had a new king, William of Normandy, William the Conqueror.

Some time before 1066 ...

On 5 January 1066 ...

The next day ...

The Events of 1066

- William landed at Pevensey in Sussex.
- Earl Harold was crowned king.
- A comet was seen in the sky.
- Harold had promised to help William become king of England. Harold swore an oath while touching the bones of saints.
- The Norwegian army landed in the north but it was beaten by Harold at the Battle of Stamford Bridge in Yorkshire on 25 September.
- The Normans beat the English at the Battle of Hastings. Harold was killed.
- King Edward the Confessor died.
- William started to prepare his ships and his army.

How do we know about 1066?

That was a story about the Battle of Hastings in 1066. The events of the battle and the result are true but we don't know if there really was someone called Thorold in the English army. We certainly don't know what he thought. Did you expect to find a story like this in a history book? Many people would be surprised because they expect history books to be boring, containing only facts that we are certain about.

History cannot be just about facts because there are many things that we are not certain about. This is because the sources – documents or other remains from the past – don't always tell us the whole

truth. They may miss events out or disagree about why things happened. Then we have to puzzle over what really happened, which can be fun! On these pages are two examples of puzzles about the events of 1066.

The Bayeux Tapestry – the full story?

The story of 1066 is told most excitingly in the Bayeux Tapestry. The tapestry was made before 1082 on the orders of William's brother. It gives lots of details about William and Harold and how William won at Hastings, but does it tell the full story of 1066?

Now work on your own or in groups, to answer the questions below.

On 28 September ...

THE FULL STORY?

1. Which event in the list goes with which scene in the Tapestry?
2. Which event is *not* shown in the Tapestry?
3. How do we know about the missing event if it is not in the Bayeux Tapestry?
4. Why do you think the Tapestry does not tell the full story of 1066?

When he heard that Harold had been crowned ...

In April ...

The Bayeux Tapestry was made in England about fifteen years after the invasion. It was almost lost during the French Revolution when it was used as a cover for a cart.

Was William the true king of England?

King Edward the Confessor had no sons or other close relatives. Before he died he probably chose someone to be the next king. But who did he choose? Below are two stories – one Norman, one English.

The English Story

Harold Godwinson, Earl of Wessex, had no royal blood but he was the most powerful man in England. After 1066 an English monk called Florence of Worcester wrote that 'Harold, who had been named by King Edward as his successor, was chosen as king by the chief men of all England. On the same day Harold was crowned by Aldred, Archbishop of York'. The Anglo-Saxon Chronicle (which was also written by a monk after 1066) said 'Earl Harold succeeded to the kingdom of England, just as the king had granted it to him and as he had been chosen as king. And he was crowned king'.

The Norman story

'Many truthful people who were there say that Harold swore on oath – of his own free will – that he would make sure that William would become King of England after the death of Edward. Later there came the bad news that England had lost its king, and Harold had been crowned. This headstrong Englishman didn't wait for the English to acclaim him as King. No – he broke his oath by gathering together a gang of his evil supporters, and seized the throne on the very day of Edward's funeral, when everyone was sad at their loss. He was crowned king by Stigand in a ceremony that was not acceptable to God. The Pope had just ordered that Stigand should no longer be a priest'.

(William of Poitiers wrote this account between 1071 and 1076. He was William's chaplain. You can also see this story in the Bayeux Tapestry)

On 14 October 1066 ...

DIFFERENT STORIES

1 How do they differ about who Edward chose?

2 What other differences can you find in the stories?

3 Both stories were written after 1066. Why do you think they were written?

4 Explain why it is difficult to be certain who Edward wanted to be king.

Were there many changes during the Middle Ages?

Later on in this book you will find more stories and more problems to investigate. In fact the whole book is an investigation. You are going to investigate what life was like in Britain after 1066, during the time we call the Middle Ages.

The main question in your investigation is 'did life stay the same or change during the Middle Ages?'.

Today everything changes very quickly. When your grandparents were young hardly anyone had a television, a car or travelled abroad. But in the Middle Ages people lived just the same kinds of lives as their grandparents and even their grandparents' grandparents. Or did they?

Answer the questions below by yourself or in groups. This will help you to sort out an answer which you can check as you continue your investigation.

11th century priest

CHANGES IN THE MIDDLE AGES

1   Look at Clue A. How powerful was the king in 1066?
2   Look at Clue B. How important was religion in 1066?
3   Look at Clue C. How difficult was everyday life in 1066?
4   If Clues A, B and C were re-written to describe life in 1500 do you think they would say different things?
5   In the Middle Ages was there
    a a lot of change?
    b some change?
    c no change?
6   Look at the timeline below. Which events might have helped to change people's lives?

Clue B: The Priests and religion

In 1066 almost everyone went to church every week and on holy days. There was only one kind of Christianity, the Catholic Church, led by the Pope in Rome. Ordinary people had to pay taxes to their local priests and richer people gave gifts to the church.

Clue A: The King and the government

In 1066 the King of England made all the decisions about how to run the country. He did not have to take advice from anyone but he depended on the lords to bring men for his army. The King of England did not control Scotland, Wales or Ireland. Sometimes English kings even had difficulty controlling the distant parts of England.

11th century king with nobles

Clue C: Everyday Life

In 1066 nearly everyone earned their living by farming in the countryside. Some people were so poor that they would starve to death if there were bad harvests but many were better off. However, even the richer peasants were not free. They had to work on their lord's land and could not leave their village without his permission. Work was hard because people and animals were the only sources of power.

Timeline 1066–1500

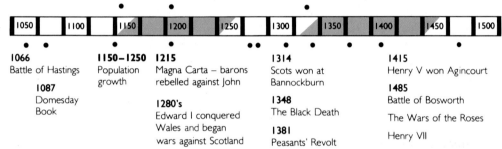

1154–1204
The Angevin Empire –
English kings held much
land in France

1337–1453
The Hundred Years
War against France

| 1050 | 1100 | 1150 | 1200 | 1250 | 1300 | 1350 | 1400 | 1450 | 1500 |

1066
Battle of Hastings

1087
Domesday
Book

1150–1250
Population
growth

1215
Magna Carta – barons
rebelled against John

1280's
Edward I conquered
Wales and began
wars against Scotland

1314
Scots won at
Bannockburn

1348
The Black Death

1381
Peasants' Revolt

1415
Henry V won Agincourt

1485
Battle of Bosworth

The Wars of the Roses

Henry VII

This timeline shows some of the main events in the Middle Ages or medieval period. The word 'medieval' comes from two Latin words 'Medium Aevum' meaning Middle Ages.

Finding the answers

When you answered question 5 you worked out an answer to your main question. It may not be completely right but it is your first idea. We call this first answer a hypothesis. As you work through this book you can improve or change your hypothesis after you have looked at the sources or other information. At the end of the book you will have a much fuller answer.

Chart of Investigation

Your INVESTIGATION	WHAT WAS IT LIKE TO LIVE IN MEDIEVAL BRITAIN?
Start with QUESTIONS	**In the Middle Ages:** Did life change or stay the same? Which was the most important event?
Work out your HYPOTHESIS	? ? ? ? ?
CHECK your hypothesis by	**INVESTIGATING SOURCES** The evidence in the sources can tell us: How people lived, what changed and what stayed the same. What affected people's lives and caused change, or continuity. How people reacted to and felt about events.
IMPROVE your hypothesis	**YOUR ANSWER TO THE INVESTIGATION**

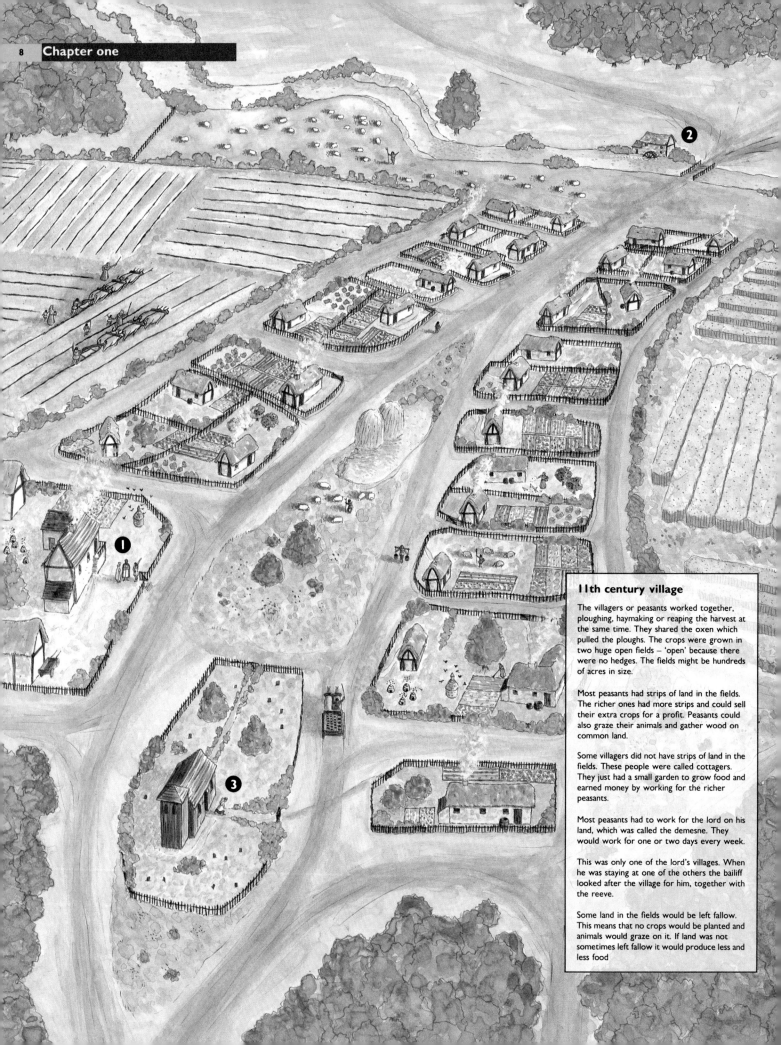

11th century village

The villagers or peasants worked together, ploughing, haymaking or reaping the harvest at the same time. They shared the oxen which pulled the ploughs. The crops were grown in two huge open fields – 'open' because there were no hedges. The fields might be hundreds of acres in size.

Most peasants had strips of land in the fields. The richer ones had more strips and could sell their extra crops for a profit. Peasants could also graze their animals and gather wood on common land.

Some villagers did not have strips of land in the fields. These people were called cottagers. They just had a small garden to grow food and earned money by working for the richer peasants.

Most peasants had to work for the lord on his land, which was called the demesne. They would work for one or two days every week.

This was only one of the lord's villages. When he was staying at one of the others the bailiff looked after the village for him, together with the reeve.

Some land in the fields would be left fallow. This means that no crops would be planted and animals would graze on it. If land was not sometimes left fallow it would produce less and less food

LIVING AND WORKING I

THE EFFECTS OF THE NORMAN CONQUEST

The first half of this book covers the years from 1066 to 1300. It will investigate how people lived and worked and the importance of the king and religion. As you find out more you will be able to check and improve your hypothesis.

❧ *Was there much change in the way people lived and worked? Did the Norman Conquest have a great effect on everyday life?*

✺ Village life

We need to start by looking at village life because nearly everyone lived in small villages. It is difficult to imagine what these villages were like. Even the picture opposite can't show you the people and animals moving, the way the colours changed each season or help you smell the countryside. However this picture does tell you some important things about life in a village in 1066. Look at the picture. Try to answer these questions, either by yourself or in groups.

Was everywhere the same?

The map below shows where there were open-field villages. Most people lived in these areas. Almost a quarter of all the people in England lived in Lincolnshire, Suffolk and Norfolk.

However people had different ways of farming in other areas, because their land was better for grazing animals than for growing crops. In these regions people lived in scattered farms so they did not co-operate like the people in the open-field villages. Each farm used its best land for crops every year. It also used another field for crops but changed this every few years.

In some places farmers also did other work. In the Mendip Hills they worked in the lead mines. In Durham they worked in coal mines. Families looked after the land while the miners were away. These men were probably better-off than people who only worked as miners, like the coal-miners of Kent and the tin-miners in Cornwall.

Proportions of village dwellers in 1066 and 1990

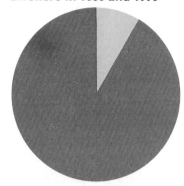

Percentage of people living in villages c.1066 – more than 90%. The total population was then about 2 million.

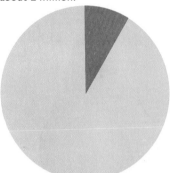

Percentage of people living in villages c.1990.

Regions where the open field system was commonly used.

VILLAGE LIFE

1 Three buildings are numbered. Which one is:
  a the mill,
  b the church,
  c the lord's house,

2 **a** How many houses are there in the village?
  b How many people do you think lived in the village? (To work this out you first have to think about how many people there might be in each family.)

3 Were all the peasants' houses the same? Describe any differences between them.

4 What kinds of work did the villagers do? What evidence is there in the picture for your answers?

5 What kinds of animals were kept and what were they used for?

6 There were two open fields in the village. Why were they called 'open fields'?

7 The lord did not work on his own land – the demesne. Who farmed it for him?

8 The two open fields were used by all the villagers. Explain how they had to co-operate with each other to make this system work.

9 What evidence is there to show that religion was important?

10 Nowadays we use gas and electricity as energy to make things work. What kinds of energy did the villagers have?

SWITHUN

The people of the village

Let's look at the kinds of people who might have lived in a village like the one on page 8.

The priest

Swithun the priest could read and write. He taught these skills to some of the village children. He also had to farm his own land (the glebe) even though the villagers paid him taxes. Each family paid one tenth of their goods (the tithe) to Swithun. Everyone went to church on Sundays and Holy Days, but Holy Days were also holidays for enjoyment.

The thegn

Before the Battle of Hastings the thegn or lord of our village was Thorold. His wife was Aelgifu. Thorold owned several villages. He had been given them in return for military service and other work that he did for the king. Thorold and Aelgifu spent time at each of their villages to see that everything was running smoothly. Like other Anglo-Saxon women, Aelgifu could inherit her husband's lands if he died and their son was still young. She could also keep land given to her by her father.

The families

Edward rented his land from the thegn. He paid rent in money and goods, such as pigs or hens. Most importantly he had to work on the lord's land every week. Some villagers, like Godric the Reeve, were better off than Edward. Godric was the most experienced farmer and had been chosen to be the reeve. This was a difficult job. The reeve had to make sure that the villagers did their work on the thegn's land (the demesne), but he also had to defend them if the thegn tried to make them work too much.

Everyone had to work. The village people started their day when the sun rose and went to bed at dusk. If the harvest was good they lived well. If it was really poor, they might starve. Everyone had to make payments of money or animals to the lord when a son married, a man died or if they wanted to leave the village for good. Some villagers had special skills so, in addition to their farm work, they worked as blacksmiths, bakers or tailors. Few villagers made their own clothes.

The women of the village worked in the fields and spent time brewing ale, baking bread and spinning and weaving cloth as well as making cheese and butter and looking after their families. Children copied their parents because they had to work too. Youngsters collected wood or scared birds, older children shepherded flocks or helped with ploughing. At harvest-time both young and old scoured the fields for small gleanings of corn while the harvesters, both men and women, reaped and stacked the sheaves.

THOROLD

AELGIFU

ALFRED

GODRIC   EDITH

EDWARD

HILDA   LEOFWYN

EMMA

NEWS OF THE CONQUEST

1 How has the information on pages 8–10 changed your ideas about whether everyday life was easy or difficult?

2 Sooner or later the news of the Battle of Hastings reached this village. What might the villagers have thought when they heard this news?

3 Who do you think would be most affected by the Norman Conquest?

Did the Norman Conquest change everyday life?

Sixty years after the Battle of Hastings a Norman monk called Orderic Vitalis wrote that:

'around 1070 peace reigned over England. The English and the Normans lived peacefully together and intermarried. Many markets were filled with French goods and the dress of the English had completely changed.'

It sounds as if there had been a lot of change and that it had been peaceful. Was Orderic right? Read the sources on pages 11–13 and then answer the questions below.

Source A

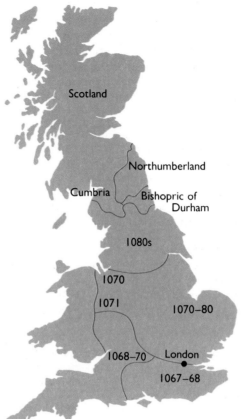

Scotland

Northumberland

Cumbria

Bishopric of Durham

1080s

1070

1071

1070–80

1068–70 London

1067–68

This map shows how the Normans gradually took over the lands of the Anglo-Saxon thegns. The first change many villagers noticed was that they had a new lord. Many thegns, like Thorold, had been killed in battle. Others simply had their land taken away and given to one of William's Norman knights. By 1086 only two Anglo-Saxons were major landowners. The heirs of Saxon thegns, like Aelgifu and Alfred, often kept some land but now they were just like other Saxons, the servants of their Norman masters.

Source B

Ordinary villagers had a new name after 1066. They were called villeins, which is from the Latin word "villani". This really just means a villager but it soon came to mean an unfree peasant so the word "villein" was a sign that the English had new masters. Many who had been free before were now villeins.

11th century peasant

CHANGES: THE EFFECTS OF THE NORMAN CONQUEST

1 Look at Sources A–G. Make a list of the effects of the Norman Conquest on the English people.
2 **a** Choose one change from your list that happened quickly.
   b Choose one change from your list that happened slowly.
3 Were all English people affected by these changes? Explain your answer.
4 Why do you think the changes in sources A,C and G happened?
5 Read source H. Do you think these events caused more problems for

villagers than the Normans had?
6 What do Sources I and J tell you about English attitudes to the Normans?
7 Make a list of everyday things which were not affected by the Normans. Look back to pages 8–10 for some ideas.
8 Do you think that the Normans had a great effect on the way English people lived? Explain your answer.
9 Do you think that Orderic's description was accurate? Explain your answer.

Source C

After the Conquest the English began to give their children French names, like John and William, Alice and Mathilda, Richard, Robert and Geoffrey. Is this surprising? The chart shows how many landowners in Winchester had foreign names. Winchester was the centre of government. Was it likely to be typical of the whole country?

Many French words were also added to English, like those listed below: baron, archer, dinner, sausage, gravy, supper, realm, roast, tax, crime, moat, portcullis, duke.

Do they tell us anything about the effects of the Conquest?

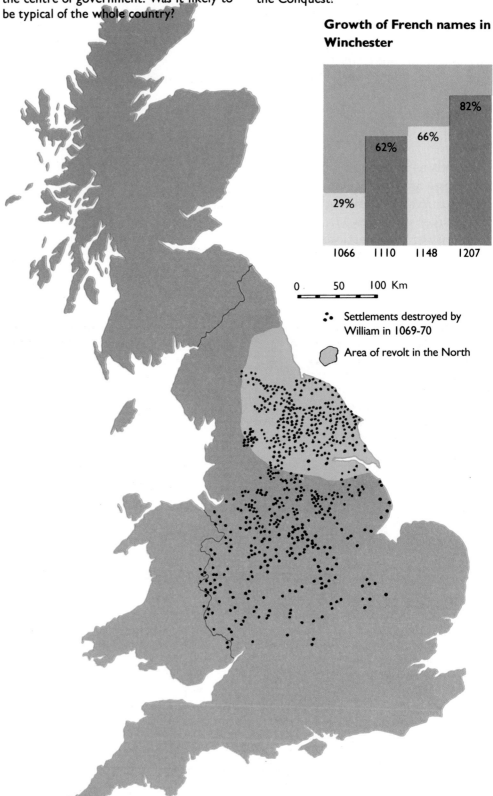

Growth of French names in Winchester

29%	62%	66%	82%
1066	1110	1148	1207

0   50   100 Km

∴• Settlements destroyed by William in 1069-70

Area of revolt in the North

Source D

The Harrying of the North

There were rebellions in several parts of England against the Normans. The most dangerous years were 1069–70 when there were risings in the south-west, on the Welsh border, in the Fens (led by Hereward the Wake) and the north. William decided to teach the English a lesson and destroyed many villages. Domesday Book in 1086 recorded many villages that were "waste" – deserted and unfarmed but this can be misleading. Many villages in the hills were probably empty because the people had been moved by their lords to better land in the lowland villages. These lowland villages were really the ones that had been destroyed in 1069–1070 but by 1086 they were again being farmed so they were not recorded as waste.

Source E

... it was horrific to see human corpses rotting in the houses and the roads. No-one was left to bury them, all having died by the sword or starvation or having fled on account of the famine. For nine years there was nobody to cultivate the land and a great silence fell all over the land. There was no village inhabited between York and Durham.

(A description of the effects of the 'Harrying of the North' written by a monk, Simeon of Durham, in the early 1100's)

Source F

The king and the chief men loved gold and silver and did not care how sinfully it was obtained. The king gave his land for as high a rent as he could but if a second man offered more then the king gave the land to him. If a third man then offered even more the king would give the land to the man who paid most and did not care how sinfully the reeves got the money from the poor.

(Anglo-Saxon Chronicle for 1087)

Source G

'In the City of York one district has been laid waste for the castle'. In Lincoln '166 residences were destroyed because of the castle'. 'At the king's first arrival in England the town of Dover was burnt. Its value could not therefore be reckoned.'
'In Shrewsbury the Earl's castle has taken over 51 dwellings.'

(Extracts from Domesday Book, a record of the whole country made by the Normans in 1086)

Source H

'1078 – And this year there was a dry summer and fire spread across many shires and burned down many villages and towns.'
'1086 – It was a very severe and sorrowful year. There was cattle plague and corn and crops did not grow. There were great problems with the weather – thunderstorms and lightning killed many people and it kept on getting worse and worse. May God Almighty make things better when it is his will.'

(Anglo-Saxon Chronicle)

Source I

After the Conquest the English secretly laid ambushes for the Normans whom they distrusted and hated and, when the chance came, they killed them. If a Norman was found murdered all the people of the region had to pay a large sum of silver as a fine – the murdrum fine.

(Extract from the Dialogue of the Exchequer written c. 1178 by Richard FitzNigel, Bishop of London)

Source J

William, king of the English, made a survey of the whole of England ... other investigators followed the first. Men were sent into areas which they did not know, and where they were themselves unknown, in order to check the first survey. The land was troubled with much violence arising from the collection of royal taxes.

(Extract from a note describing the Domesday Survey made by Robert Losinga, Bishop of Hereford from 1079–1095)

The Anglo-Saxon Chronicle was begun in c.890, perhaps on the orders of King Alfred. It was a record of the main events in England. At first there was just one account but then monasteries began to add their own versions to their copy so by 1066 there were several different Chronicles with slightly different information in them. Each year's events were written down shortly afterwards but nobody knows exactly how long afterwards.

Motte
A mound with a tower that could be defended against attack

Bailey
The outer area where soldiers lived and kept their stores

Moat
An area dug to make the castle harder to attack. It might be full of water

A motte and bailey castle
These simple castles were built by the Normans to defend themselves and frighten the English. There were only a handful of castles in England before 1066 and they had been built by Edward the Confessor's Norman advisers. Soon after 1066 there were wooden castles in all the main towns. Why do you think they were made of wood?

LIVING AND WORKING 2: 1100–1300

A TIME OF IMPROVEMENT

The Norman Conquest changed the lives of many people, but change continued over the next 200 years. During this period many people became richer and lived more comfortably.

≈ Was there much change in people's lives?
Why did everyday life improve?

Castles are a good source of evidence. After 1066 many motte and bailey castles (like the one on page 13) were built. Gradually castles changed. They were built of stone instead of wood. They became much larger and towers were added to the walls. The strongest castles were on the Scottish border and in Wales, because of threats of invasion and revolt.

However, there were other kinds of changes in castles. Some became more like homes than military bases because the kings won more control and made England more peaceful.

Landowners were rebuilding in style in the 1200's with separate areas for the family away from the servants. There were more wall hangings and possessions. This picture is of Stokesay Castle.

Keeps like this were built in the twelfth century. Was it still more of a military base than a home?

THE DEVELOPMENT OF CASTLES

1 Look at the castle on page 13. What evidence is there that it was a military base, not a home?

2 Look at the picture of the keep. What evidence is there of this castle as:
   a a military base?
   b a home?

3 Look at the picture of Stokesay castle. In what ways is this more like a home than a castle?

4 How do the changes in castles help to show that England was becoming richer and more peaceful?

The lives of many ordinary people also improved. They had more to eat. The basic diet was coarse, dark bread, oatmeal pottage and weak ale. They did not eat much meat, but the better-off villeins ate cheese, milk and eggs and could afford to buy a greater range of foods. Vegetables and fruit — such as apples, pears, cabbages, onions and garlic — grew in villagers' gardens.

Landowners also had more choice of food. They ate white bread as their staple food. They could also afford to buy large amounts of fresh meat and fish and they drank wine. Wine, dried fruits and spices became more common for the rich, but they looked down on ordinary fruit and vegetables. Can you think why? Did the landowners have a better diet than the peasants?

Some things, however, did not change. Life was hazardous and always short. Many children died before they were five years old. Those who reached the age of 20 could expect to live to about 40. Wealthier people might live up to ten years longer. Many women, rich or poor, died in childbirth. Farming accidents could lead to disability or death from blood-poisoning. Disease was spread by vermin and water. Poor harvests could lead to starvation so people risked food-poisoning by eating rotten meat or mildewed crops. After long winters and food shortages many people died in April and May.

There was a greater quantity and variety of clothing for all. Villeins had always tried to use good cloth but had saved by not dyeing it. Now they used more colours. The better-off had linen underclothes, furs and many more items of clothing

None of this would change until people could understand or treat diseases effectively. However, between 1066 and 1300 more food and a slightly better diet helped to fight off sickness. Babies were stronger because their mothers were better fed.

The simplest houses were built of mud, wood and thatch. They measured perhaps 10m × 5m. Richer peasants had long houses like this one, perhaps 30m × 5m.

By the 13th century stone was used more often, either as a base or for full walls. Houses had solid doors and shuttered windows but open hearths made them dark and smoky. Houses were thoroughly swept — archaeologists have found the hollows made by brooms!

Changes in prices between 1175 and 1350

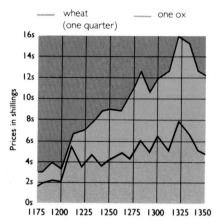

Why do you think prices went up sharply in some years?

Peasant Landholdings 1279–80

Free peasants

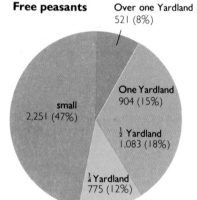

Over one Yardland 521 (8%)

One Yardland 904 (15%)

½ Yardland 1,083 (18%)

¼ Yardland 775 (12%)

small 2,251 (47%)

Total: 5,534 free peasants

Villeins

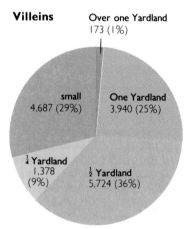

Over one Yardland 173 (1%)

One Yardland 3,940 (25%)

½ Yardland 5,724 (36%)

¼ Yardland 1,378 (9%)

small 4,687 (29%)

Total: 15,902 villeins

A yardland was about 30 acres, enough to feed a family comfortably. Records from 1279–80 show that peasants did not all have the same amount of land. What percentage of peasants were still not free? If there was a bad harvest would many be in danger of starvation?

⊜ More freedom and new towns

Another important change was that more villeins became freemen. By 1300 many villeins paid a cash rent for their strips instead of working for their lord. The lords agreed to this. It was easy for them to hire labourers for a low wage. Villeins also moved away from their home village to find work in other villages or in towns. Again lords agreed. They could find new tenants who would pay higher rents for land.

The landowners profited most of all from these changes. Villeins also did well if they had plenty of land and could sell their extra crops. However the poor continued to struggle and by the late 1200s conditions had become very

This map shows the new towns which were founded between 1066 and 1334. Can you think of any reasons why there were hardly any new towns in the south east and East Anglia?

difficult for them. More people died with each bad harvest because they had not recovered properly from earlier shortages.

Many people who bought their freedom moved to towns. Suddenly there were many more towns. Some just grew out of villages but many were completely new. Kings, lords or bishops built these towns to encourage trade and make themselves richer. At the same time old towns, like York,

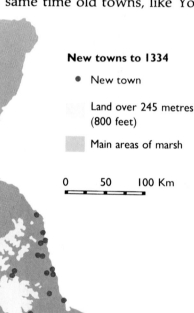

New towns to 1334

● New town

Land over 245 metres (800 feet)

Main areas of marsh

0   50   100 Km

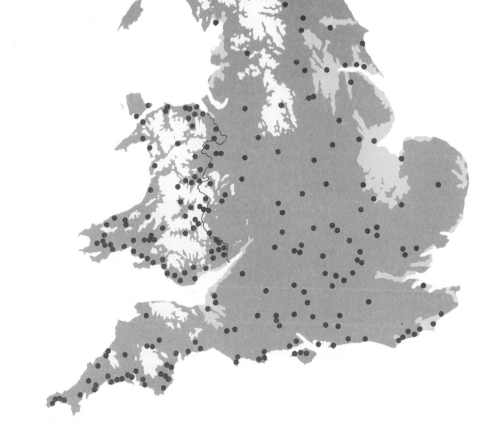

doubled in size.

To us these medieval towns would have seemed very small and very countrified. There were fields of crops outside the town walls where the townspeople grew food. However farming was less important than trade. Carlisle was not a very large town, but its people traded many items: wool, hides and skins; cloth, linen and leather; iron and copper, wax, charcoal and timber; dyes for clothworkers as well as fish and all kinds of animals and crops.

In the towns the people were free of ties like working on their lord's demesne. If they worked hard they might do well. But life in towns was still risky. Not everyone could find work and so there was still the danger of hunger. Towns were unhealthy places. Houses were crowded closely together. The streets were often full of rubbish and dirt and there were plenty of rats to spread disease. It was not easy to get fresh water or to keep it fresh. There was more crime than in the villages, even though the town gates were closed at night for security. Would you have moved to a town from the countryside?

Towns and guilds

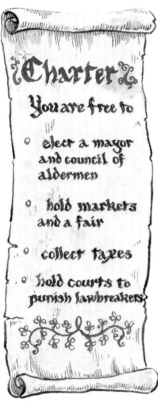

The king could get money by selling a charter and he also received a payment from the town each year.

Richard I and John sold many charters to gain money for their wars.

The townspeople could decide many things for themselves once they had a charter. The men who owned property in the town were called burgesses and they elected the council.

All towns wanted to buy a charter from their lord because a charter gave them freedom. Many towns bought charters between 1100 and 1300.

Charter

You are free to

○ elect a mayor and council of aldermen

○ hold markets and a fair

○ collect taxes

○ hold courts to punish lawbreakers

CHANGES: THE WAY THEY LIVED 1100–1300

1 What changes were there in the way people lived between 1100 and 1300?
2 Which of the phrases below best describes the changes in everyday life?
  important improvements
  some improvement
  very little change
  Explain the reasons for your answer.
3 a The changes in List A helped to improve the lives of the rich. Explain how these changes were connected.
  b The changes in List B helped to make the lives of the poor more difficult. Explain how these changes were connected.
4 This chapter is called 'A Time of Improvement'. Do you think that is a good way of describing the years 1100 to 1300? Explain your answer.

List A

Landowners sold crops for higher prices

Landowners had a more varied diet

Landowners had better housing

List B

Food cost more money

Rents for land were higher

There were more deaths from starvation

English population 1100–1340

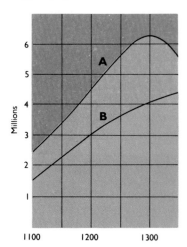

Historians cannot be certain how many people lived in England in the Middle Ages. Line A shows the highest estimates. Line B shows the lowest estimates. Whatever the truth was, we know the population increased rapidly.

Temperature changes

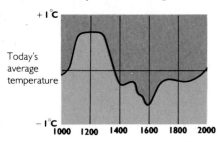

This chart shows how the weather became warmer between 1100 and 1300, helping farmers grow more food and people become healthier.

◉ Why was everyday life changing?

Although life for the poor was still very difficult, many peasants had better housing, clothing and more food. Many had bought their freedom. Landowners were even wealthier. Why had these changes happened?

One important cause was that the population doubled between 1100 and 1300. When there were more people there was more trade and higher prices for food.

Another reason was that more land was being used for farming. Lords started new villages. They cut down woodland, drained marshes and fens and cleared hillsides, so that more food could be grown. Some lords even moved all the houses in a village onto wasteland to free land for growing crops.

This was also a time of good weather for farmers. The summers were warm and there were few severe frosts to damage the crops. This was why more high land was used for farming, higher in the north of England than in any later century. Even vineyards flourished. Of course there were still bad harvests but there were far fewer in the 1200s. There were only 12 bad harvests between 1208 and 1299 but 22 between 1300 and 1399.

One way to produce more food was to change the way fields were used. Look at the plans of the two-field and three-field systems and answer the following questions:

2 field system

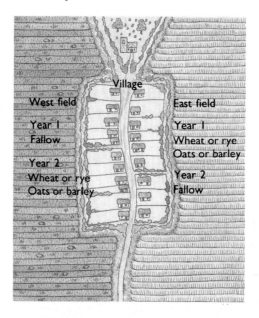

3 field system

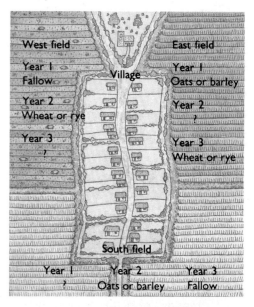

FIELD SYSTEMS

1 Why was land left fallow?
2 In the three-field system:
  a What would the East field be used for in Year 2?
  b What would the West field be used for in Year 3?
  c What would the South field be used for in Year 1?
3 **a** How much land was left fallow in each year in the two-field system?
  b How much land was left fallow in each year in the three-field system?
4 Many villages changed from the two-field to the three-field system in the 12th and 13th centuries. Why did they change?
5 What other evidence is there on these pages that people needed to grow more food?

In some areas, like Warwickshire, people used a four-field system with legumes (peas and beans) as the fourth crop. Many landowners read books on farming. The most famous book was by Walter of Henley. He gave advice on fertilisers, crops, breeding and culling animals. Other changes were the increased use of horses instead of oxen and the building of more windmills.

Despite all these efforts it was increasingly difficult to feed all the people. There were no machines to make work quicker and more efficient. The amount of food farmers could produce stayed low. Today the same amount of seed produces three times more wheat or barley.

CAUSES AND CONSEQUENCES: WHY DID LIFE CHANGE BETWEEN 1100 AND 1300?

1 Make a list of the **causes** of change in everyday life.
2 Historians divide causes into **long-term** causes and **short-term** causes.
   a What do you think the difference is between these kinds of causes?
   b Can you find one long-term cause and one short-term cause in your list.
3 Which of the causes you have listed did the most to change people's lives? Explain your answer.
4 Why couldn't people grow enough food to feed everybody in the late 1200s?

SUMMARY

Changes in everyday life 1066–1300

Here is a list of the changes in everyday life that happened between 1066 and 1300.

- New towns
- Freedom for more people
- Foreign lords
- Castles built
- More land used for farming
- Saxon thegns lost land
- Better housing and diet
- Many new words
- Changes in farming methods
- Many homes destroyed after rebellions

1 On the right are two flow charts. Copy them and then fill in the gaps by linking the changes to the correct causes.
2 Look at the two flow charts. Do you think that the Norman Conquest had more effect on everyday life than the changes in population and climate? To help you decide think about how many people were affected and which changes lasted the longest.
3 You have investigated many changes, but many things did stay the same. Here is a list of these continuities.

- Almost everybody still worked as farmers
- The fastest way to travel was on horseback
- Many people still faced starvation if the weather was bad
- The only power came from people and animals

Compare this list with your lists of changes. Which of these two sentences do you agree with? Explain your answer.

a Everyday life changed a great deal between 1066 and 1300.
b Everyday life stayed very much the same between 1066 and 1300.

Flow charts

The Norman Conquest

More people better weather

THE POWER OF THE KING I: 1066–1300

Clue A
Coins

There was one system of coins for the whole country. These silver pennies were only made at special mints by men who were appointed by the king. The kings also had a very careful system for recording and collecting taxes.

Clue B
Law and order

Anglo-Saxon kings made laws for the whole country. In every shire the shire-reeve's job was to make sure that people kept the king's laws. However the earls who owned large areas of land could become more powerful than the shire-reeves if the king was weak.

Clue C
Royal travels

Some Anglo-Saxon kings did not travel far from Winchester, their capital city between 900 and 1066. They used their thegns and earls to rule the country. Other kings, who were usually good soldiers, did travel to distant parts of England.

Clue D
The Northumbrian rebellion, 1065

In 1065 the people of Northumbria rebelled against their earl, Tostig. Why did they do this? The *Anglo-Saxon Chronicle* records that it was because Tostig 'robbed God and took life and lands from all those weaker than himself'. Another source says that 'another cause was that Tostig had taken heavy taxes from the whole of Northumbria'.

Although Tostig had been chosen by King Edward, the Northumbrians chose a new earl. He was Morcar, the brother of Earl Edwin of Mercia. Then the Northumbrians marched south to meet the king to make certain that he accepted Morcar as their Earl.

The King was the most important person in the country. His job was to defend the country and keep law and order. People believed he was chosen by God and that he could even heal the sick by touching them.

🐍 *Did the power of the king change between 1066 and 1300?*

You can keep a record of your investigation and check your hypothesis by copying and filling in the grid below.

This grid will help you to record the evidence about the power of the king. For example, if you decide that William the Conqueror increased the power of the king then tick the top box in column **A**.

	A William the Conqueror	B Domesday Book	C Feudalism	D Magna Carta	E Parliaments
The power of the king **INCREASED**					
The power of the king **FELL**					
The power of the king **STAYED THE SAME**					

☰ The power of the Anglo-Saxon kings

Before we can find out whether the power of the king changed we need to know how powerful they were before 1066. Did the Anglo-Saxon kings control the whole of England? Three possible answers are given in the grid below. Draw your own grid to help you decide. Tick answer 1, 2 or 3 for each of the four clues. Then decide which answer you agree with.

	ANSWERS	Coins	Law and order	Royal travels	Northumbrian rebellion
1	All Anglo-Saxon kings could control the whole of England				
2	Anglo-Saxon kings could not control the whole of England				
3	Some kings could control the whole of England				

William the Conqueror

Some Anglo-Saxon kings could rule the whole country. Their main problem was controlling the furthest parts of the kingdom. But even the northerners accepted being governed from the south, provided the government was fair. When William became king in 1066 he made changes so that he was even more powerful than the Anglo-Saxon kings.

The two accounts below give different views of the way William governed the country after 1066. Read them and then answer the questions below.

William the Conqueror

William had been Duke of Normandy since he was seven. As a child he saw plots and murders. Two of his guardians were assassinated before he began to rule Normandy himself, aged 17. His first task was to deal with revolts in Normandy. He was still only 20 when he won his first great battle and crushed the rebels. After that William became one of the strongest rulers in Europe, even before he conquered England.

The power of the king was very different from today. How do the powers of today's monarch match William I's?

Account A
After God had given him victory King William gave the lands of England to his faithful knights. The king had to make sure that the country was safe from rebellions. He replaced most of the English sheriffs and bishops with Normans. He had castles built in all the main towns to give security to his soldiers and punished those who rebelled against their rightful king. In 1085 William ordered the Domesday survey so that he could govern and collect taxes more efficiently.

Account B
After he won the Battle of Hastings the King took the land of the English and gave it to his Norman knights. He also replaced nearly all sheriffs and bishops with foreigners. He built castles to frighten the people and destroyed the land of those who fought back against the newcomers. William ordered the Domesday Survey so that he could find out how much he could take from the people.

The king was God's representative. This was shown by God giving William his first victory at Hastings

The king needed the support of his barons to control the country, especially in the north and south west

William owned all the land. Everyone, even barons, depended upon him for their land

The power of William the Conqueror

The king made all the decisions even though he asked others for advice. However he did not have to consult anyone

The king had the power of life and death over everyone. He could decide any law case and punishment

The king was more powerful because he controlled England and part of France

Everyone was expected to fight for the king

DIFFERENT VIEWS: WILLIAM THE CONQUEROR

1 List 3 differences between Accounts **A** and **B**?
2 Which account might have been written by an Englishman and which by a Norman? Explain your answer.
3 There are both **facts** and **opinions** in these accounts. List one fact and one opinion from each account.
4 Which of these accounts do you think is correct? Explain your answer.
5 What evidence would you use to show that William was more powerful than the Anglo-Saxon kings?
6 Now fill in column A of your grid.

≋ Domesday Book

In 1085 the Danes threatened to invade England. At Christmas King William had 'very deep discussion' with his council. William realised that he needed to know exactly who owned land and what each village was worth. This information would help him to collect more taxes or feed more of his soldiers in future. William ordered a great survey of England that we call *Domesday Book*. Domesday Book is a good example of William's power in his new country.

The Domesday Survey covered all England except Cumbria, Durham and Northumberland. The rest of the country was divided into regions and a different group of commissioners visited each region. Everywhere the commissioners asked the same questions. The most important questions were:

● Who holds the land?
● How much land is there?
● How many villeins, cottagers, freemen and slaves are there?
● How much woodland, meadow and pasture is there?
● What is the land worth?

Each question had to have three answers — one for before 1066, one for the year when William gave the land to its owner and one for 1086, the year of the survey.

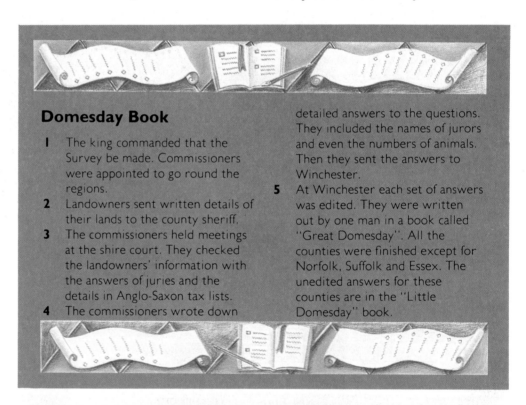

Domesday Book

1 The king commanded that the Survey be made. Commissioners were appointed to go round the regions.
2 Landowners sent written details of their lands to the county sheriff.
3 The commissioners held meetings at the shire court. They checked the landowners' information with the answers of juries and the details in Anglo-Saxon tax lists.
4 The commissioners wrote down detailed answers to the questions. They included the names of jurors and even the numbers of animals. Then they sent the answers to Winchester.
5 At Winchester each set of answers was edited. They were written out by one man in a book called "Great Domesday". All the counties were finished except for Norfolk, Suffolk and Essex. The unedited answers for these counties are in the "Little Domesday" book.

DOMESDAY BOOK

1 What can a historian find out about life in Norman England from *Domesday Book*?
2 Was collecting information from the people a completely new idea? Explain your answer.
3 How does the Domesday Survey show that William was very powerful?
4 The writer of the *Anglo-Saxon Chronicle* said that the Domesday Survey was 'shameful'.
  a Why do you think English people criticised the survey?
  b How might a Norman have answered the English criticism?
  c Would a historian today agree with the English or the Norman ideas about *Domesday Book* or neither? Explain your answer.
5 Now fill in column B of your grid.

🅂 Feudalism

Feudalism was a very important part of medieval life but it is a complicated idea to explain in words. It is much easier to show you what it was, so the activity on this page will only work if you take part! Here's what you have to do:

1 Divide into groups of five. One of you must be the king, one an earl, one a knight and two villeins. Stand or sit in a row, as you can see in the diagram.

2 Feudalism is a word describing how people were linked together. The answers to these questions will show you how the feudal system worked.

   a Look at the chart below. Work out what you would have had to do for the people next to you. For example, if you are a knight what do you have to give the earl and what do you give the villeins?

   b If the king asks for a very high relief, where does the earl get the money from?

   c If the king is going to fight a long war abroad would he be better asking for scutage from the earl or taking him in the army?

3 How did feudalism make kings more powerful after 1066?

4 Now fill in column C of your grid.

Historians argue whether the Normans began feudalism in England. In many ways Anglo-Saxon England was feudal. The king gave land to his thegns in return for service. The thegns gave land to peasants in return for work. However the Normans did add two new features to feudalism – knights, soldiers who were trained to fight on horseback with lances, and castles.

The chart below makes the feudal system look very neat but it soon began to change. Strong kings made their own rules. If they wanted to ask for a higher relief than usual from an heir there was no-one to stop them – unless there was a rebellion.

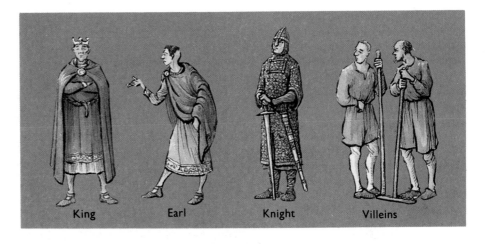

King   Earl   Knight   Villeins

The Feudal System

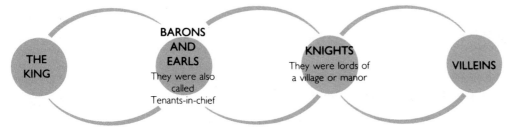

The king promised to rule fairly and take advice from his barons. He gave them land to support their followers.

The barons gave land to their knights and defended them if they had quarrels.

The knights gave land to their villeins so they could grow their own food.

THE KING

BARONS AND EARLS
They were also called
Tenants-in-chief

KNIGHTS
They were lords of a village or manor

VILLEINS

The barons brought men to fight for the king for 40 days a year. The more land they had, the more men they brought. They had to pay a tax called a relief to inherit their land and to pay a tax if the king's son was knighted or his eldest daughter married. If a baron did not want to fight he had to pay a tax called scutage (shield money).

The knights served in the baron's army for 40 days a year or served in one of his castles. They also had to pay a relief to inherit their lands and a tax when the baron's son was knighted and his eldest daughter married.

The villeins worked on their lord's land one or two days a week. They paid a heriot (usually their best animal) to inherit their land, a marchet when their son married and a chevage if they wanted thei freedom to leave the village.

Magna Carta – a fall in royal power?

King John 1199–1216. John was the son of Henry II and the younger brother of Richard I, who was king from 1189–1199.

What happened in John's reign

1199	John became king
1203	John's nephew and rival, Arthur, was captured and murdered
1204	The French won back their lands in northern France
1206	John quarrelled with the Pope and the Pope ordered that no church services should be held in England
1213	The French beat John's army at the Battle of Bouvines
1214	The rebellion began and the French invaded England
1215	Magna Carta seemed to end the barons' rebellion
1216	John died

Henry II (1154–1189)

Henry II who made great changes to the system for holding courts and finding criminals

Henry II and his sons, Richard I and John, were always looking for new ways of increasing their power. Over the years these kings took more and more money from their barons to pay for the government of their huge empire.

The barons could not complain because the kings were their feudal lords and because Henry II and Richard were very powerful. However after 1210 John was faced by many problems. He was quarrelling with the Pope and had lost Normandy to the King of France, so he needed even more money to fight back.

Some barons, who thought they had suffered the most, joined together to rebel. Some had been forced to pay high taxes before they could inherit their lands. Many were northerners who did not want to fight or pay for the French wars which were so far away from their own lands.

Not everyone rebelled. Just as many barons were on the king's side. To stop a civil war the two sides met at Runnymede on the Thames and made an agreement – the Magna Carta. The panel below shows seven of the 63 clauses (or sections) of the Magna Carta:

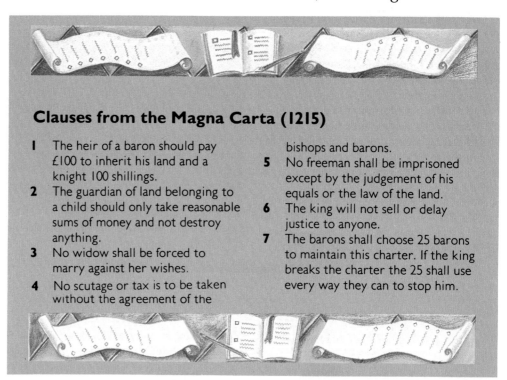

Clauses from the Magna Carta (1215)

1 The heir of a baron should pay £100 to inherit his land and a knight 100 shillings.
2 The guardian of land belonging to a child should only take reasonable sums of money and not destroy anything.
3 No widow shall be forced to marry against her wishes.
4 No scutage or tax is to be taken without the agreement of the bishops and barons.
5 No freeman shall be imprisoned except by the judgement of his equals or the law of the land.
6 The king will not sell or delay justice to anyone.
7 The barons shall choose 25 barons to maintain this charter. If the king breaks the charter the 25 shall use every way they can to stop him.

DIFFERENT VIEWS: MAGNA CARTA

1 Look at the clauses of Magna Carta. How had John been raising the money he needed?
2 Nicholas Stuteville paid £6000 to inherit his land. He overpaid – by how much?
3 Choose clauses from Magna Carta that would support these statements:
   a Magna Carta protected the barons against the king.
   b Magna Carta made sure everybody was treated fairly by the law.

4 People often think Magna Carta was important because it protected ordinary people. Do you think this idea is correct?
5 Which clause do you think
   a was most important to the barons and
   b the king most objected to?
   Explain your answers.
6 **a** Write down two facts about King John.
   b Write down two opinions of your own about King John.
7 Now fill in column D of your grid.

Parliaments – could they control the king?

The Lords

King

Archbishop of Canterbury

Archbishop of York

Great landowners

Court officials

Lords

The Commons met separately from the Lords and included two citizens from every important town and two knights from every shire.

Magna Carta did not stop the civil war. John had only agreed to buy time and he soon attacked the rebels. Even the Pope said that John did not need to keep the agreement because kings were God's representatives. Their power could not be limited. Only John's death saved England from a long civil war.

That was not the end of Magna Carta. It was re-issued while John's son, Henry III, was young. It became the basis for many laws and the way the king should treat his barons. However, Henry III did not keep to these ideas.

In the 1250s there was another civil war about the king's power. The barons wanted to make certain that Henry took advice from all the barons and not just from his special favourites. Led by Simon de Montfort the barons set up a council of 15 men. These men, together with another 12, would meet three times a year to hold discussions – or parliaments.

Henry III thought that he had lost his power and that it was his duty to God to fight back. Eventually de Montfort was killed at the Battle of Evesham in 1265 but this did not end parliaments. Kings had a use for them.

Edward I often needed money for wars. He had to get men from each shire to agree to the taxes. The easiest way to do this was to call all the shires together when the king was holding a parliament or discussion with his barons.

Henry III (1216—1272)
He became king when he was only nine years old

THE BEGINNING OF PARLIAMENT

1 Why did the barons try to control the king in 1215 and the 1250s?
2 What methods did they use to control the king?
3 Why did these attempts to control the king fail?
4 Why did parliaments start to meet regularly?
5 Now fill in column E of your grid.

Summary: The power of the King 1066–1300

Look at the grid you have filled in.
a How had the king's power changed?

b Draw a new version of the diagram on page 21 to show the power of the king in 1300.

ENGLAND AT WAR I: 1066–1300

Family tree of the Scandinavian kings of England

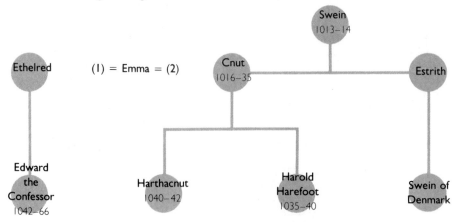

The Norman Conquest increased the power of the king in England. Later, other kings tried to increase their power even further until the barons rebelled. Between 1066 and 1300 English kings also tried to increase their power over the rest of Britain.

✎ Did England take control of the rest of Britain?

First we need to look at something that definitely changed in 1066. Look at the family tree and Sources A and B and then answer the questions.

Source A

1066 – Harald Hardrada, the King of Norway, came with 300 ships up the Humber to York. Earl Morcar and Earl Edwin fought against them and the Norwegian king had the victory. King Harold came with a great force of Englishmen and met him at Stamford Bridge and killed him.

(*Anglo-Saxon Chronicle*, describing events in September 1066)

Source B

1070 – King Swein came from Denmark into the Humber and the local people came to meet him and made a truce – they expected that he was going to conquer the country. Then the English people from all the Fenlands came and expected that they were going to conquer all the country. The two kings, William and Swein, came to an agreement but the following summer the Danish fleet came into the Thames and lay there for two nights.

(*Anglo-Saxon Chronicle*, 1070)

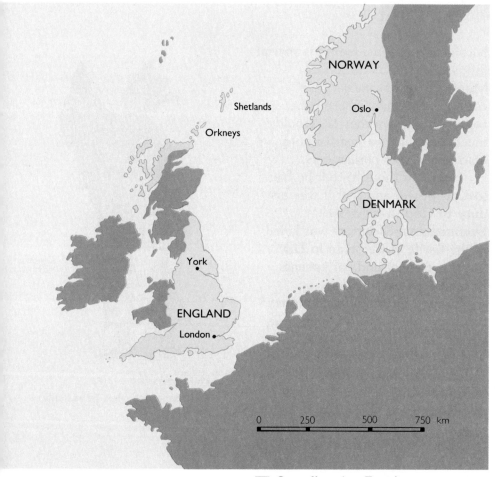

Scandinavian Empire

ENGLAND AND EUROPE

1 Which empire did England belong to between 1016 and 1042?
2 Did Scandinavian interest in England end in 1042? Explain your answer.
3 How dangerous were attacks from abroad after 1066? Explain your answer.
4 Was it inevitable that England became part of the Norman Empire?

♒♒♒♒ Britain in 1066

The events of 1066 altered England's connections with Europe, but did they affect the rest of Britain? First we need to find out about Britain before the Normans arrived. Look carefully at the map below.

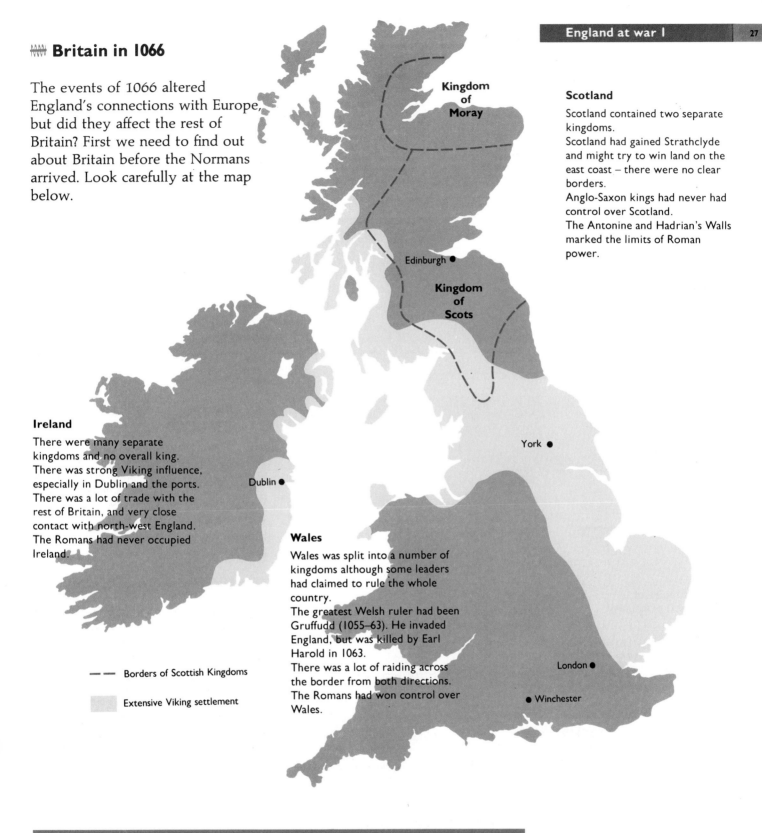

Scotland

Scotland contained two separate kingdoms.
Scotland had gained Strathclyde and might try to win land on the east coast – there were no clear borders.
Anglo-Saxon kings had never had control over Scotland.
The Antonine and Hadrian's Walls marked the limits of Roman power.

Ireland

There were many separate kingdoms and no overall king.
There was strong Viking influence, especially in Dublin and the ports.
There was a lot of trade with the rest of Britain, and very close contact with north-west England.
The Romans had never occupied Ireland.

Wales

Wales was split into a number of kingdoms although some leaders had claimed to rule the whole country.
The greatest Welsh ruler had been Gruffudd (1055–63). He invaded England, but was killed by Earl Harold in 1063.
There was a lot of raiding across the border from both directions.
The Romans had won control over Wales.

- - - Borders of Scottish Kingdoms

Extensive Viking settlement

BRITAIN IN 1066

1   Before 1066 Kings of England claimed to be the lords of all Britain. How much of Britain did they really control?
2   Do you think that William was most likely to interfere in:
   a   Wales?
   b   Scotland?
   c   Ireland?
   Explain the reasons for your answer.
3   Do you think that Wales, Scotland and Ireland would be able to resist a Norman invasion?

	Wales	Scotland	Ireland
William the Conqueror 1066–1087	Norman barons quickly took control of lowland Wales and by 1075 had taken all the good farming land. Further progress was stopped by the mountains. William did not visit Wales until 1081.	William attacked Scotland in 1072 following a Scottish invasion of England. He forced King Malcolm to accept him as overlord. Later Scottish kings invaded England and won land. Scotland stayed independent.	William did not attempt to invade Ireland.
Henry II 1154–1189	Henry claimed to be overlord of Wales but did not really control the mountain kingdom of Wales.	Henry captured William the Lion of Scotland in 1174. William had to give up land in England and surrender Scottish castles to Henry. He agreed that Henry was his overlord but Scotland really stayed free and independent.	Henry sent barons to take land in Ireland and, in 1171, went to Ireland himself. All the Irish kings accepted him as their overlord but his power was, in reality, quite limited.

The Empire of Henry II of England

All four Norman kings ruled Normandy as well as England. The Plantagenets brought Anjou and Aquitaine (both in modern France) into this 'empire' too. So until the thirteenth century, English kings spent only part of their time in England as Henry I's movements show.

- Land Henry II inherited from his father
- Land Henry II inherited from his mother
- Lands Henry II acquired by marriage
- Lands largely under Henry II's control

Changes in Britain – 1066–1200

Between 1066 and 1200 English kings tried to win control over more of Britain. How successful were they? Answer the questions below, using the information in the grid.

THE POWER OF ENGLAND

1 Was Scotland or Wales more successful in resisting William I? Explain your answer.
2 Why do you think William did not invade Ireland?
3 Do you think that the Normans ever meant to conquer the whole of Britain?
4 Henry II already had a large empire. Why did he want to control more of Britain?
5 Did William I or Henry II have more power over the rest of Britain?
6 Do you think that English kings had much effect on people in the rest of Britain?

✳ Edward I – lord of all Britain?

Henry II was an energetic and aggressive king. He ruled a large empire but also wanted to prove that he was the overlord of all Britain. However Scottish kings and Welsh and Irish princes were able to keep their own laws and rule their lands in their own ways. Even the strongest English kings did not have the money or men to control all Britain directly.

This situation changed in the reign of Edward I (1272–1307). Wales lost its independence. Scotland had to fight a series of wars to keep its freedom. As you read the next two pages think about this question: Why was Scotland more successful than Wales in resisting Edward?

Edward I and Wales

Wales was not one country but a lot of small kingdoms. In the 1200s this changed because the princes of Gwynedd took control of other areas. In the Treaty of Montgomery (1267), Llywelyn was accepted as Prince of Wales by the English. However this treaty was made when there was civil war in England.

When Edward I became king Llywelyn refused to kneel in front of Edward and accept him as his overlord. In 1277 Edward invaded Wales to prove his power. Helped by Welsh enemies of Llywelyn, he quickly defeated the Welsh prince. However Edward let Llywelyn remain as Prince provided he accepted Edward as overlord.

Five years later Llywelyn fought back and this time Edward set out to bring Wales completely under his control. Llywelyn was killed in 1282 and his brother, Dafydd, was executed. Edward built powerful castles to keep control, especially in the rebellious north.

In 1284 Edward made a law (the Statute of Wales) saying that he had taken full control of Wales. Many English laws were introduced and Wales was split into counties controlled by English officials. In 1301 Edward I's son became 'Prince of Wales' – a great insult to Welshmen who remembered Llywelyn.

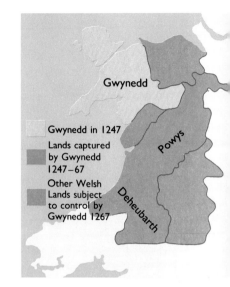

The growth of Gwynedd in the thirteenth century

Edward I, shown on his seal

Conway Castle in North Wales, built by Edward I

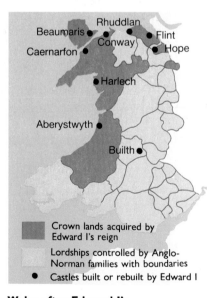

Wales after Edward I's conquest

The Battle of Bannockburn

Edward I at his coronation

Edward I and Scotland

Although some Scottish kings accepted English kings as their overlords this had no effect on their own powers or actions. Scotland was too powerful and too far away to be conquered and controlled by England. At times the Scots won control over parts of the north of England but for many years there was peace.

In 1286 Alexander III died, leaving his only grand-daughter, Margaret, as his heir. However Margaret drowned, ending Edward's plan to marry her to his son. There was disagreement about who should be king and Edward was asked to settle the dispute. The two main candidates were John Balliol and Robert Bruce.

Edward chose John Balliol as king, then he insisted that Balliol accept him as overlord and that Scottish law cases should be decided in England. The Scots would not accept this but their army was beaten by Edward at Dunbar in 1296. Afterwards, Edward took the Scottish royal documents and the Stone of Scone, on which Scottish kings had been crowned, to England.

Gradually the Scots won back their freedom. They kept fighting, led first by William Wallace and later by Robert Bruce. Edward led several campaigns, but the size and mountains of Scotland, Bruce's guerilla tactics and the Scots' desire for freedom meant that Edward could never be successful.

After Edward I died the Scots were even more successful. In 1314 they won a great victory over the English at Bannockburn and in 1328 the English accepted Robert Bruce as King of Scotland. The Scots had kept their freedom.

Now are the islanders all joined together
And Scotland reunited to the royalties
Of which King Edward is proclaimed lord.
Cornwall and Wales are in his power
And Ireland the great at his will.
There is neither king nor prince of all the countries
Except King Edward, who thus has united them.

These were the words of the chronicler Peter of Langtoft, soon after Edward I's death in 1307. Was he right? Did the people in the rest of Britain agree?

In 1320 the Scottish nobles sent a letter known as the Declaration of Arbroath, to the Pope which contains these lines:
'One hundred and thirteen kings of our royal line have reigned, unbroken by a single foreigner. Our people lived free until Edward, king of the English, molested our kingdom. The wrongs that he did cannot be understood unless you had experienced them. We have been delivered by our lord king Robert. As long as a hundred men are left we will never submit to the power of the English. It is not for glory, riches or honour that we fight but only for liberty.'

The Welsh had finally been beaten by English pressure. Since 1066 much of Wales had been settled by lords from England and there had never been united resistance to the English. Finally, Edward I had conquered the

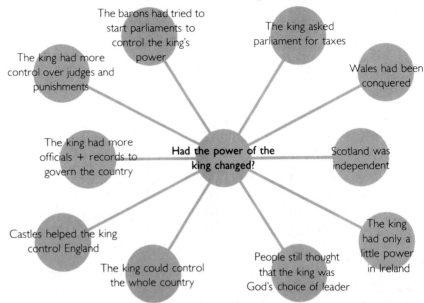

The power of the king 1066–1300

The barons had tried to start parliaments to control the king's power

The king asked parliament for taxes

The king had more control over judges and punishments

Wales had been conquered

The king had more officials + records to govern the country

Had the power of the king changed?

Scotland was independent

Castles helped the king control England

The king could control the whole country

People still thought that the king was God's choice of leader

The king had only a little power in Ireland

remaining parts of Wales. However, Welshmen recalled in the Chronicle of Princes (*Brut y Tywysogyon*) the great day of Gwynedd when:
'the King granted that the Prince should be obeyed by the barons of Wales and that there should be Princes of Wales from that time forward.'

Only small areas of Ireland were closely controlled by England. Other areas were held by lords who had come from England. Law cases from these areas were often decided at Westminster and taxes were collected for the English kings' wars. However most of Ireland was free from English rule. Ireland was not rich or troublesome enough to be invaded. It is unlikely it could have been conquered.

A thirteenth century English view of the Irish and of the Welsh

SUMMARY: England at war: 1066–1300

1 Did England's power over the rest of Britain increase or fall between 1066 and 1300?
2 Below are three reasons why England could not conquer Ireland and Scotland. Which reason was the most important?
   a distance
   b costs
   c opposition from the local people
3 Look at the pictures on the right. How might the English have been drawn by the Scots, Welsh or Irish?

RELIGION AND THE PEOPLE

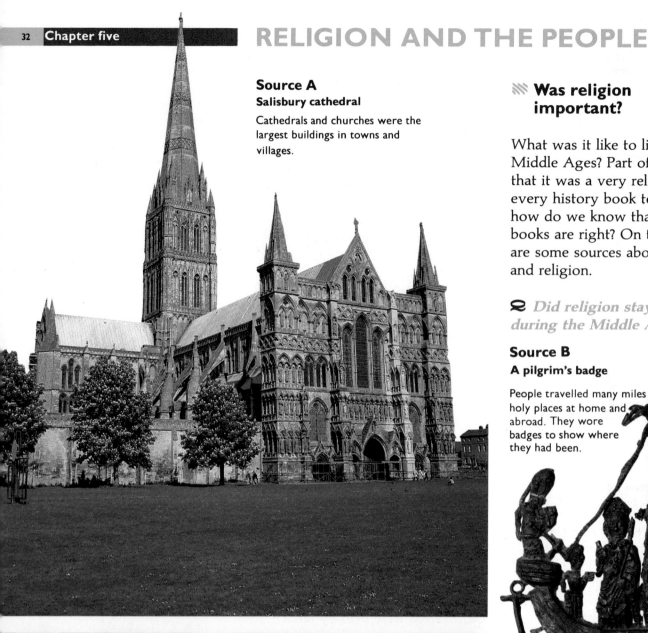

Source A
Salisbury cathedral

Cathedrals and churches were the largest buildings in towns and villages.

Was religion important?

What was it like to live in the Middle Ages? Part of the answer is that it was a very religious time — every history book tells us so. But how do we know that the history books are right? On these pages are some sources about churches and religion.

Did religion stay important during the Middle Ages?

Source B
A pilgrim's badge

People travelled many miles to holy places at home and abroad. They wore badges to show where they had been.

Source C
Demons taking the wicked to hell. A stained glass window in Canterbury Cathedral

Source D

Mon.	Sept. 8	Nativity of Blessed Virgin Mary	paid
Mon.	Sept. 29	St. Michael	unpaid
Sat.	Oct. 18	St. Luke	paid
Tue.	Oct. 28	St. Simon and St. Jude	unpaid
Sat.	Nov. 1	All Saints	paid
Tue.	Nov. 11	St. Martin of Tours	unpaid
Thu.	Nov. 20	St. Edmund King and Martyr	paid
Tue.	Nov. 25	St. Katherine	unpaid
Sat.	Dec. 6	St. Nicholas	paid
Mon.	Dec. 8	Conception of Blessed Virgin Mary	unpaid
Thu.	Dec. 25	Christmas Day	unpaid
Fri.	Dec. 26	St. Stephen	unpaid
Sat.	Dec. 27	St. John the Evangelist	unpaid
Mon.	Dec. 29	St. Thomas of Canterbury	unpaid

(Holidays of Roger of Langley during the last four months of 1337. He was a skilled carpenter employed at the Tower of London — other holy days were taken as holidays by other craftsmen.)

Source E

A scene from a Morality play.
The martyrdom of a Saint

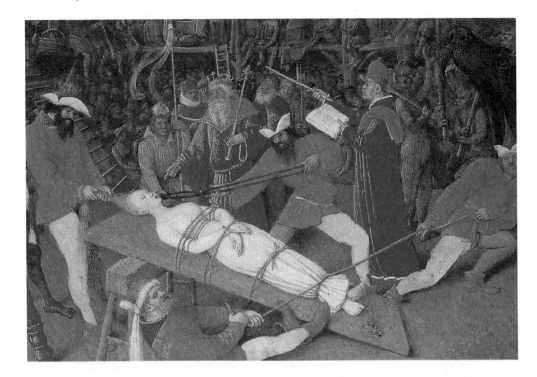

On holidays people watched plays based on stories from the Bible or on religious events. The plays showed how Good beat Evil or warned people that they would go to hell if they were sinners. This scene of the death of a saint showed that people should love their religion enough to die for it.

Heaven or hell?

HEAVEN
Only the saints went straight to heaven to live with God

PURGATORY
Most people had to spend some time in purgatory to be punished for their sins. They hoped that they would be allowed into heaven sooner if they had been on pilgrimages, paid for church buildings or been good to other people.

HELL
Evil people went straight to hell where they were tormented by devils for ever.

Source F

For marble, freestone from Caen and Reigate, ragstone, plaster, chalk and for carriage of these ...   **£459 12s 9d**
For heavy timber, boards, beams, hurdles, grease, glue and for carriage of these ...
                                                           £53 15s 11d
For lead, iron, steel, charcoal, locks, ropes, glass, wax, pitch, and for making cement and for carriage of these ...   **£140 14s**
For the wages of masons, carpenters, painters, plumbers, glaziers, and messengers ...   **£670 5s 10d**

(From the accounts for building at Westminster Abbey from December 1269 to February 1271. At the time a skilled worker was paid 3d per day.)

Source G

Old Romney – William the Chaplain has a certain Agnes, his sister so they say, in his house. In the church there are no books, the chalice needs repair, the font has no lock, the roof of the chancel and the church are in bad condition.

Eastbridge – the vicar did not appear and he has never lived there nor was a chaplain found. The people of the parish asked for a good priest.

(Extracts from the records of the Archbishop of Canterbury for 1292–4. The Archbishop's men visited the parishes in his diocese to check the priests and the churches.)

EVIDENCE: WAS RELIGION IMPORTANT?

1 Look at Sources A, B and D. Explain what each of these sources tells us about religion in the Middle Ages.
2 Look at all the sources on these pages. Which of them would help you investigate:
   a church buildings
   b complaints against the church
3 Which of these statements is correct?

   a Religion was not important in the Middle Ages
   b Religion was quite important in the Middle Ages
   c Religion was very important in the Middle Ages
4 Which source or sources were most helpful in answering question 3? Explain your choice.

Monasteries

Numbers of monasteries

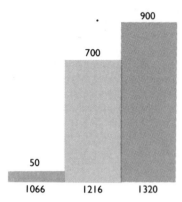

Year	Number
1066	50
1216	700
1320	900

In the late 13th century there were
- 12,500 monks
- 7,000 nuns

1 person in every 150 was a monk or a nun.

In addition about 40,000 other people worked for the monasteries as servants

Another sign that religion was very important was the number of monasteries. More and more were built in the Middle Ages. The chart shows you how many monasteries there were and how many monks and nuns.

How did they live?

As you can see from the timetable, the main work of monks and nuns was to pray. In between prayers they spent time working in the abbey. Some wrote out books by hand, with beautiful coloured pictures called illuminations.

Monks also had to help people. Many abbeys were in towns and the monks gave gifts of food or money to the poor. They also gave them medicine and gave shelter to travellers.

Many monasteries became very rich. People thought that giving land or money to the church would help them go to heaven when they died. The monks also earned money by keeping sheep on their land and selling the wool in England and abroad. The money was used to build finer churches or buy treasures for inside the church.

A monk's day – summer

Time	Service
2.00 a.m.	Nocturns
Daybreak	Matins
6.00 a.m.	Prime
8.30 a.m.	Tierce
11.30	Sext
12.00	**Meal**
14.30	Nones
17.30	**Meal**
18.00	Vespers
20.00	Compline
20.15	**Bedtime**

Work had to be done between Matins and Compline.

Benedictines

Benedict had been a monk and he wrote a set of rules about how monks should live. Most monks were Benedictines in the 10th and 11th centuries. Many Benedictine monasteries were built in England before 1066.

Franciscans

These men were not monks living in monasteries. They thought that they ought to live more like Jesus, travelling round the country talking to people about God. The first Franciscan was St. Francis and he told his followers that they should have no possessions. St. Dominic began another group called the Dominicans. The people called these wandering preachers "friars". The first friars came to England in 1221.

Cistercians

As time went by some monks began to change St. Benedict's Rule. Other monks did not like these changes and said that they wanted to get back to a simpler life. These monks began new orders. The first of these was at Citeaux in France, which is where the word Cistercian comes from. Many Cistercian Abbeys were built in England in the 1100's, including Fountains, Rievaulx and Kirkstall.

THE DEVELOPMENT OF MONASTERIES

1 When did the number of monasteries grow most quickly?
2 Why did new orders of monks begin?
3 Why did the friars think they were more religious than the monks?
4 How did monasteries affect the lives of ordinary people?

%%% Kings and the church

All medieval kings were involved with the church. They spent money on building cathedrals and abbeys. They also expected to control bishops and priests, just like they controlled everything else in the country.

When William the Conqueror became king he replaced English bishops and abbots with foreigners. Some English bishops became involved in rebellion against William so he decided that he could not trust them. When an English bishop died he was replaced by a Norman or someone else that William knew he could trust. One Norman abbot even brought archers into his church to force the monks to use a different kind of service.

Later there were quarrels between kings and the churchmen. One argument was over church law. Anyone who was a churchman could escape severe punishment by having his case heard in a church court.

Henry II tried to change this – and he seemed to have a good

chance because the Archbishop of Canterbury was his old friend, Thomas Becket. Becket had been Henry's chief adviser before the king made him Archbishop. Unfortunately, Becket did not help his old master. He stood up for the church against the king. Becket was murdered by four of Henry's knights. Later Henry showed his sorrow.

The Normans rebuilt many English churches and cathedrals in the Norman style. This helped to show the English that the Normans were their new masters. Norman churches were much larger with enormous pillars and arches. However, this style was not completely new in England. Edward the Confessor had built Westminster Abbey (below in the Bayeux Tapestry) in this style.

KINGS AND THE CHURCH

1 Why did William the Conqueror want to manage the bishops and abbots?
2 Why did Henry II want to change church law?
3 Why is the evidence on this page useful for showing that religion was important in the Middle Ages?

The monks could hear the knights coming towards them as they sat with the Archbishop, Thomas Becket. The Archbishop did not seem to notice. He went on talking even when the knights entered the room. Staring straight at Becket the knights demanded that he obey the king's orders.

'If all the swords in England were aimed at my head, your threats would not change my mind', said Becket, 'I am surprised you dare to threaten an archbishop'.

'We will do more than threaten', replied their leader. And then they turned and marched out.

Some monks were shaking with fear but they all begged the Archbishop to run or hide. Then they heard the sound of an axe on wood. Someone had closed the hall door and the knights, returning with their supporters, were breaking it down.

The monks pushed and pulled their archbishop towards the church but he would not hurry. He walked slowly, with the Cross of our Lord carried in front of him. He was near the altar when the knights burst in. All the monks fled, except Robert, William and Edward. The four knights, covered in armour from head to foot, moved towards Becket with their swords drawn.

'Where is the traitor?' one shouted. Becket took no notice.

'Where is the Archbishop?' asked another.

'Here I am, said Becket, 'No traitor, but a priest of God. I marvel that you have entered the church of God clothed like that. What do you want with me?'

'Your death', the knights replied. 'It is impossible that you should live a moment longer.'

One of them struck the Archbishop with the flat of his sword and they started to drag him away from the altar.

The three remaining monks pulled Becket back. Then a knight raised his sword and struck. Edward put out his arm to defend his Archbishop. The sword cut deeply into Edward's arm and then wounded Becket in the head. Wiping away the stream of blood the Archbishop gave thanks to God, saying, 'Into Thy hands, O Lord, I commend my spirit.' As he knelt down a second blow struck him on the head and he fell. While he lay there another struck him with such force that the sword broke. Thomas Becket, Archbishop of Canterbury, was dead.

Did Henry II order Becket's murder?

After the Archbishop's death people blamed King Henry II. The four knights had come from Henry's court in France. It would have been easy for Henry to order his men to kill his enemy.

Read Sources **H** to **L** below and answer the questions to help you to solve this puzzle – did Henry order the knights to murder Becket?

Source H

No-one is so good-tempered and friendly as the king. Whenever he goes out he is seized upon by crowds and pulled hither and thither but he listens to everyone with patience. He does not show any anger but when he is hustled beyond bearing he silently goes to some quiet place.

(Walter Map – a member of King Henry's court who wrote in the 1180s)

Source I

The king's eyes are dove-like when he is at peace but gleam like fire when his temper is aroused. In bursts of passion they flash like lightning. He never sits down except when on horseback or at meals and he always has his weapons in his hands when not working or at his books. When he relaxes he reads or debates with his officials.

(Peter of Blois, King Henry's secretary for some years)

Source J

Except when troubled in mind or moved to anger he was a great prince and, remarkably, good at reading and languages. He was wrong to try to gain power over the church. He joined together the laws of the church and the king out of ignorance as well as enthusiasm for justice. He spent scarcely an hour at church services and even then spent most of the time in discussions rather than prayer.

(Gerald of Wales, a member of Henry's household for many years)

Source K

It was said to the king that the Archbishop was going around England at the head of a strong army. One of his councillors said, 'My lord, while Thomas Becket lives, you will have neither peace nor quiet nor see good days.' At this the king felt such fury, bitterness and anger against Becket that it was obvious to all around. Four knights, seeing his anger and keen to win his favour, left the court, having sworn to kill the Archbishop.

(William Fitzstephen, a priest in Becket's household who wrote around 1175 but was not present at this conversation)

Source L

There is no doubt that the king was at first wholly ignorant of the knights' flight. After it had been discovered the king gave orders to stop them.

(G. W. Greenaway, *The Life of Thomas Becket*, 1961)

Becket was murdered in Canterbury Cathedral in December 1170. Immediately, pilgrims began to visit his tomb and people said that miracles happened there.

EVIDENCE: THE MURDER OF BECKET

1   Read Sources **H** and **I**. Do they agree or disagree about the king's temper?

2   Does Source **J** agree or disagree with Sources **H** and **I** about the king's temper?

3   What questions would you ask about the writers of Sources **H**, **I** and **J** to find out if they were accurate?

4   Which of Sources **H**, **I** or **J** is likely to be the most accurate about the king's temper?

5   Is Source **K**'s account likely to be accurate, given what you have read in Sources **H**, **I** and **J**?

6   Look at all the sources. Do you think that Henry ordered the knights to murder Becket?

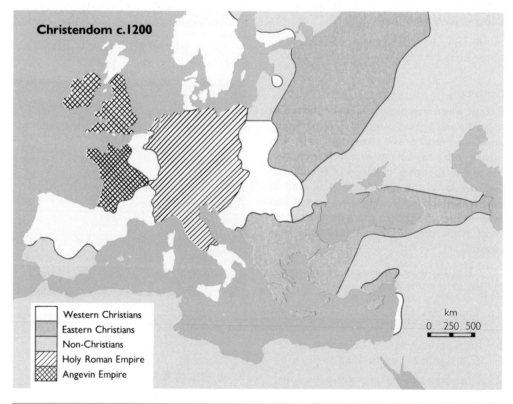

Pilgrims travelled all over Europe and some even went to Jerusalem. The Crusaders thought of themselves as partly pilgrims and partly soldiers.

Christendom – christians united

Everyone hoped that they would go to heaven after they died. They knew that they would have to spend some time in purgatory first but this would not be too long if they had been good and religious. Therefore religion was important to each and every person.

Religion was also important to kings and their countries because religion linked the countries of Europe together. Nowadays countries have people from all kinds of religions but in the Middle Ages everyone in Europe was Christian. They were all members of the Catholic Church and the Pope was the head of their church. All the Christian countries together were called Christendom.

Sometimes the countries of Christendom could work together. The most famous examples are the Crusades – the Wars of the Cross. The Christians wanted to win back their Holy City, Jerusalem, from the Moslem armies. However, Jerusalem was also a Holy City for the Moslems so they were just as determined to win.

In the end the Crusades failed, partly because the different kings could not work together. Perhaps this wasn't surprising. They were often at war with each other over land. King John even quarrelled with the Pope over who should choose the Archbishop of Canterbury. The Pope punished the whole of England. All church services had to stop. If people died without being baptised or confessing their sins they would not go to heaven. Eventually, John had to give in.

Christendom c.1200

Legend:
- Western Christians
- Eastern Christians
- Non-Christians
- Holy Roman Empire
- Angevin Empire

km
0   250 500

WAS CHRISTENDOM UNITED?

1 Which countries were part of Christendom?

2 Why do you think that kings could join together in a Crusade even though they had been fighting each other in Europe?

3 Why did King John quarrel with the Pope when they were both leaders of Christendom?

4 Do you think that Christendom was an important idea in the Middle Ages? The timeline on page 39 may help you.

Was religion always important?

In this chapter the evidence told us that religion was very important to people in the Middle Ages. They did not save religion for Sundays. It was part of their everyday lives. The church provided most of the schools. It looked after the sick and poor. Holidays were really 'holy-days' so people could always remember when each saint had his or her day.

However, we need to ask another question – 'Did religion stay important throughout the Middle Ages?' After all, 500 years is a long time for something to stay the same.

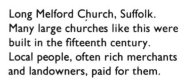

Long Melford Church, Suffolk. Many large churches like this were built in the fifteenth century. Local people, often rich merchants and landowners, paid for them.

J. Wycliffe 1330–1384
Wycliffe said:

The Church must give up its wealth.

The Bible should be in English so all can read it.

People should not have to pay the tithe to the Church.

Churchmen should live in poverty and rely only on charity.

There is no point in worshipping holy relics, such as the bones of saints.

Bread and wine do not turn into the body and blood of Christ during church services.

Timeline of Crusades

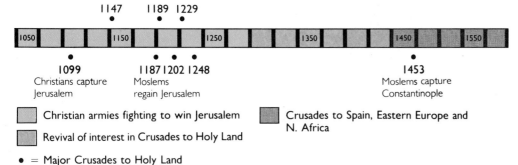

1147   1189 1229

| 1050 | | | 1150 | | | 1250 | | 1350 | | 1450 | | 1550 | |

1099
Christians capture
Jerusalem

1187 1202 1248
Moslems
regain Jerusalem

1453
Moslems capture
Constantinople

☐ Christian armies fighting to win Jerusalem

☐ Revival of interest in Crusades to Holy Land

☐ Crusades to Spain, Eastern Europe and N. Africa

● = Major Crusades to Holy Land

WAS RELIGION ALWAYS IMPORTANT?

1 Did religion stay important throughout the Middle Ages? Which sources give the best evidence to support your answer?

2 Look back to the other sources in this chapter. Do they give evidence to support or alter your answer to question 1?

In the fifteenth century some people who said that the Catholic Church's ideas were wrong were burned to death as heretics – unbelievers. Which of these ideas would be most heretical?

Were there many changes during the Middle Ages?

In the introduction you were asked whether there was change in the Middle Ages. Your task then was to suggest answers, using just a little information and the ideas you already had. Since then you have been investigating what life was like in Britain between 1066 and 1300 and thinking a little more about your answer. These two pages sum up your investigation so far and give you the chance to look again at your answer or hypothesis. Can you improve your hypothesis and give evidence to support it? Here is an example of how the investigation might have worked.

Which events affected people's lives?

Richard

(first idea)
'The Norman conquest because the Normans took over the country and built castles.'

(second idea)
'The changes in population and climate were more important than the Norman Conquest. The Normans changed a lot but the changes in population and climate affected everyone and changed everyday life.'

The effects of kings' ambitions and wars
- Changes to the laws and ways of finding criminals
- The conquest of Wales and part of Ireland
- The first meetings of parliaments
- Civil wars with their barons
- The growth and then loss of an empire
- More castle building
- Higher taxes

Effects of the Norman Conquest
- Houses and villages were destroyed in some places
- The king had more power in England and some control over Wales
- Many people lost their freedom
- England had closer links with France instead of Scandinavia
- English landowners and bishops were replaced by foreigners
- New words and names were used
- Castles and new cathedrals were built

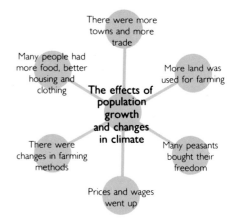

The effects of population growth and changes in climate
- There were more towns and more trade
- Many people had more food, better housing and clothing
- More land was used for farming
- There were changes in farming methods
- Many peasants bought their freedom
- Prices and wages went up

These are just examples. You may not agree with them. What are your answers now?

Many things did change in the Middle Ages. You have just been thinking about some of them. But was there a lot of change or did the most important things stay the same? Look at the diagram opposite.

CHANGES AND CONTINUITIES

1 List:
  a the changes
  b the continuities – the things that stayed the same.
2 Do you think there had been:
  a a lot of change
  b some change

  c no changes at all
3 What evidence would you use to support your answer?
4 Which events had the most effects on people's lives? (Do you agree with Richard?)

The population total had doubled

Living conditions had improved for many people but by 1300 many were again in danger of starving

Nearly everyone still lived in country villages

Scotland was still a free and independent country

The King controlled England much more firmly

Change or continuity 1066–1300

Kings still took all decisions but were expected to listen to advice from their nobles and call parliament if taxes needed

Religion was still very important for everyone

Many people had bought their freedom

Many new towns had begun to grow

The King of England controlled Wales and part of Ireland

Did life change or stay the same?

Kate
(first idea)
'Life stayed the same.'
(second idea)

'There was quite a lot of change. There were more people, castles were built, parliaments began and England won control of Wales.'

In this investigation you have been working like a historian, using historical skills and ideas. you will have learned some things about the work of historians. Can you answer the questions below about how historians work?

HISTORICAL SKILLS AND IDEAS?

1 **a** List 4 kinds of sources of evidence that tell us about medieval Britain?
   b Do historians always believe the information in written sources? Explain why or why not.
2 'Even an important event only has one cause.' Do you agree? Give reasons for your answer.

3 'Historians only investigate changes. They are not interested in things that stay the same.' Is this how you have worked in your investigation?
4 Historians often disagree about what happened in the past. Can you think of two reasons why they disagree?

LIVING AND WORKING 3

THE EFFECTS OF THE BLACK DEATH

Disaster!

The sun was still above the trees that grew alongside the Great Field. It was early to be stopping work when there was so much to do, but he must return home to see his father. Thomas scraped the mud off his leather boots and shouldered his wooden spade. As he walked along the grass track that led to the village Thomas thought of all the children who had played there, waiting for their parents to return from the fields. Today there was nobody playing.

When he reached the edge of the village he quickened his pace. He passed the church and turned up the slight rise to his house. Ruth, the widow who lived next door, sat outside combing wool, making use of the last of the day's light. Neither of them spoke.

Thomas walked along the side of his house. He noticed that some of the thatch had slipped. He would see to it one day — if he had time. He crouched low and walked through the doorway. The smoke made his eyes cloud over with tears but he quickly adjusted to the gloom. The fire in the centre of the room gave just enough light for Thomas to see his father lying on the straw. Alice, Thomas' wife, was stirring a pot on the fire as she sat holding their baby. The smell of onions and garlic mingled with the smell of smoke and animals. Alice told Thomas that his father had not moved all day.

His father had been coughing badly for the last four days. Now he was very weak. Thomas gently raised his father's head so he could drink a little water. There was a speck of blood at the side of this father's mouth. It was time for Thomas to look. He feared the worst. Thomas took his knife and slit his father's smock along the arm. He eased his father's arm up so that he could see more clearly.

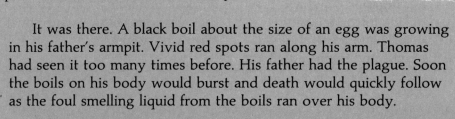

It was there. A black boil about the size of an egg was growing in his father's armpit. Vivid red spots ran along his arm. Thomas had seen it too many times before. His father had the plague. Soon the boils on his body would burst and death would quickly follow as the foul smelling liquid from the boils ran over his body.

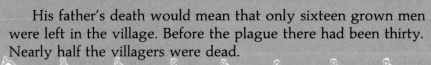

His father's death would mean that only sixteen grown men were left in the village. Before the plague there had been thirty. Nearly half the villagers were dead.

The arrival of the Black Death

The plague that ravaged Thomas's village arrived in England in the summer of 1348. During the next year it killed at least one person in every three. Later, historians called this plague the 'Black Death'. You can now investigate what happened in the years after the Black Death

✎ Did the Black Death change the way people lived in Britain?

The plague first appeared in England in Melcombe Regis (now called Weymouth). Melcombe Regis was an important port and had a great deal of trade with European countries. The disease spread quickly from the south west to Oxford and then to London. It moved north during 1349, advancing quickly in the warmer weather and pausing during the colder months.

Unfortunately, the winter of 1348–1349 was unusually mild. Even in February 1349 the plague was very active. A contemporary writer, Robert of Avesbury, recorded 'that between the second of February and the end of Easter 1349, more than 200 plague dead were buried almost every day in a cemetery newly made in Smithfield, London.'

The Dance of Death
Suddenly people were dying. Today it is difficult to imagine what it felt like to live during the Black Death unless you think about the victims of famine or earthquakes. What does this picture tell you about people's feelings?

Map showing the origins and progress of the Black Death

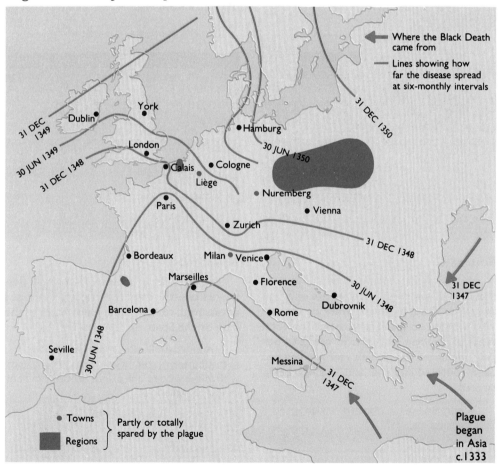

Where the Black Death came from
Lines showing how far the disease spread at six-monthly intervals

31 DEC 1349
30 JUN 1349
31 DEC 1348
30 JUN 1348
30 JUN 1350
31 DEC 1350
31 DEC 1348
30 JUN 1348
31 DEC 1347
31 DEC 1347

Dublin, York, London, Hamburg, Cologne, Calais, Liège, Nuremberg, Paris, Vienna, Zurich, Bordeaux, Milan, Venice, Marseilles, Florence, Rome, Dubrovnik, Barcelona, Seville, Messina

● Towns } Partly or totally
▨ Regions } spared by the plague

Plague began in Asia c.1333

The Black Death was carried by fleas which lived on rats. Rats on ships or hidden amongst merchants' goods, helped the disease to spread along the trade routes.

THE BLACK DEATH

1 Why was the plague called the 'Black Death'?
2 Which routes did it spread along?
3 Why did the mild winter help the plague to spread?
4 In the first half of this book we investigated
  a everyday life,
  b Kings and government and
  c religion.
Which of these three would be most affected by the Black Death?

English Population 1100–1525

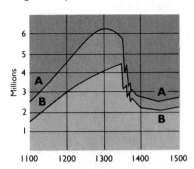

Line A shows the highest number estimated by historians.
Line B shows the lowest number. Why do you think there is disagreement?

Below: These words were scratched on a church wall at Ashwell, in Hertfordshire: '1349, the pestilence; 1350, pitiless, wild, violent; the dregs of the people live to tell the tale ...'

Right: The rich as well as the poor fell victim to the disease

The plague years
Plague continued for many years and stopped the population increasing. Later plagues killed young people who had not developed resistance to the disease. After the Black Death of 1348–9, plagues broke out again in the years 1361, 1369, 1374 and 1390.

How many people died?

The Black Death affected every part of life but its greatest effect was on the way people lived and worked. This was because so many people died that there weren't enough people to work in the fields – but how many people did die from this plague?

Source A

In the year of our Lord, 1349, the hand of God struck the human race a deadly blow. This scourge in many places left less than one fifth of the population surviving. It struck terror into the hearts of the whole world. So great a pestilence had never been seen or heard or written of before this time. So huge a number was not even swept away by the flood which happened in the days of Noah.

(Chronicle of Louth Park Abbey, written in the 14th century)

We are certain that a large number of people were killed by the plague, but it is difficult to say exactly how many. Nobody kept accurate population statistics in the Middle Ages. However, historians have found some evidence that gives us an idea of how many people died.

Source B

Man and wife with their children travelled the same road, the road of death. To stop these notable events perishing with time and fading from memory, I have set them down in writing while waiting among the dead for the coming of death. And to stop the writing perishing with the writer, I leave the parchment for the work to be continued in case in the future any human survivor should remain.

(John of Clyn, an Irish Friar, 1349)

Source C

A jury in August 1349 declared under oath that the mill was of no value, for not only was the miller dead, but there were no tenants who wanted to grind any corn. The total rents of freemen and serfs in the previous year amounted to £12. This year nothing had been collected and the land was not being farmed.

(Court Roll of the Manor of Sladen, Buckinghamshire, 1349)

Source D

... the pestilence is believed to have destroyed two-thirds of the English, but not, I am assured, to have done much harm to the Irish or the Scots.

(Archbishop FitzRalph of Armagh, writing in the fourteenth century. In areas of high land with fewer villages, the plague probably did not spread so easily.)

EVIDENCE: HOW MANY DIED FROM THE BLACK DEATH?

1 What does each of Sources **A** to **D** tell us about the number of deaths?
2 Which source or sources are most useful for investigating the number of deaths? Explain the reasons for your choice.
3 Do the sources give us useful evidence about anything other than the number of deaths?
4 Why can't historians be more exact about the number of deaths?

How did people react to the Black Death

It is very difficult to imagine how people felt while their friends and relatives were dying all around them. However the sources on page 44 told us a little about people's fears and ideas. Some people thought that the world was going to end. The sources on this page give you more information about the way people thought and behaved while the Black Death spread.

Source F
A drinking party

Source E

Some thought that by living quietly they could avoid the danger. Others believed that plenty of drinking and enjoyment, singing and free living was the best way to prevent the plague. Day and night they went from one tavern to another, drinking and carousing. They ran wild in other people's houses and there was no one to prevent them for everyone had abandoned all responsibility for his belongings as well as for himself.

(A description of life in Florence in Italy by Boccaccio in *The Decameron*, 1350)

Source G

% of London wills granting money to hospitals

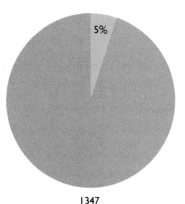

5%

1347

15%

1360

Apart from trying to help the sick why else did more people leave money in their wills to hospitals?

Source I
Death rides triumphant
(from Palermo Cathedral)

Source H
A cadaver from a tomb in Salisbury Cathedral

REACTIONS TO THE BLACK DEATH

1 Look at Sources **E** and **F**. How did some people behave at the time of the Black Death?
2 Look at Source **G**. How did other people react to the Black Death?
3 Look at Sources **H** and **I**. What do they tell us about the way the Black Death affected people's thoughts and worries?

Commutation

Many more peasants paid for their land in cash instead of by working for their lord. They had greater freedom because they no longer spent part of the week farming the lord's land. Paying cash was also less humiliating than working on the demesne. This exchange of a villein's labour dues for a money rent was called 'commutation'.

Leasing

Landowners were keen to rent or lease land to villagers rather than have it as part of their demesne. This gave the peasants the chance to acquire more land. The picture shows a leasing document.

How did working life change?

In 1300 there seemed to be too many people in England. After the poor harvests between 1315 and 1321 many people starved to death. After 1348 there were not enough people. This meant changes for the peasants and for the landowners because farming relied on people to do the work. Without people the land could not be ploughed, new crops could not be sown, nor could the crops be harvested.

In the 1360s nearly everyone still lived in villages like the one in the picture. This is the same village that you saw on page 8 but it has changed a good deal since 1066.

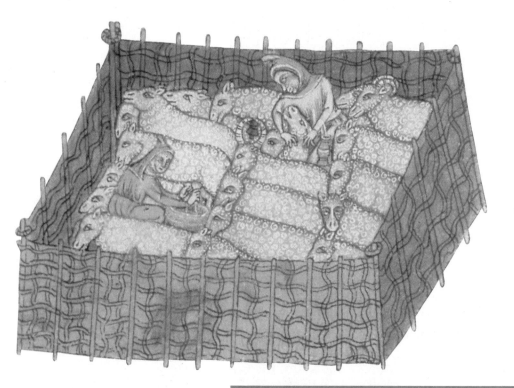

Animal Farming

More of the land in the village was used for animal farming. Sheep farming became very popular in many areas. Fields that had once grown wheat or barley were often turned into grazing for sheep.

CHANGES: FARMING THE LAND

1. Compare this picture with the one on page 8. Make a list of the things that have stayed the same since 1066.
2. Make a list of the changes that have happened since 1066.
3. Look at the rest of this page. It shows three important changes in village life in the fourteenth century.
   a How did the Black Death help to cause these changes?
   b Which people gained most from these changes?
4. Look at the sources on page 48. Does their evidence support the statements in the diagram?
5. Did the Black Death cause new changes or simply speed up changes that were already happening?

Changes at work

Source I

The plague crossed the sea coast at Southampton and came to Bristol and there almost everyone died, struck by sudden death. At Leicester in one parish more than 380 died and in another more than 400.

There were lower prices for everything because of the fear of death. A man could buy a horse worth 40s for 6s 8d. Sheep and cattle wandered through crops and there was no-one to look after them. In the autumn no-one could employ a reaper for less than 8d and his food and a mower for less than 12d and his food. There were so few priests that many church services did not take place.

(From the Chronicle of Henry Knighton, written in Leicestershire before 1366)

Source J

This graph shows the number of sheep in the flock at Watboys Abbey. Why do you think it grew so much?

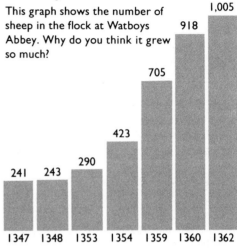

Source K

This graph shows the number of days that villeins worked on the lord's demesne in the village of Cuxham. Why did the numbers fall?

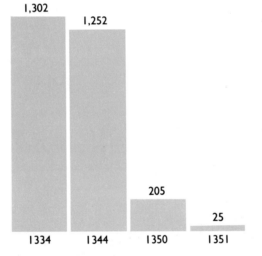

Source L

Lords often allowed free peasants to farm some of the demesne land instead of using the labour of villeins. In Broughton the lord let out 11 acres in 1344 but later the number of acres increased. Did the increase begin with the Black Death? Was there a lot of change in this village compared with the others mentioned on this page?

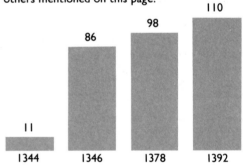

SUMMARY

How did the Black Death affect the people?

A Before 1348

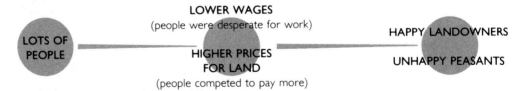

LOTS OF PEOPLE — LOWER WAGES (people were desperate for work) / HIGHER PRICES FOR LAND (people competed to pay more) — HAPPY LANDOWNERS / UNHAPPY PEASANTS

B After 1348

FAR FEWER PEOPLE — HIGHER WAGES (landowners needed to keep workers) / LOWER PRICES FOR LAND (lots of land was empty – there was more than enough to go round) — HAPPY PEASANTS / UNHAPPY LANDOWNERS

LIVING AND WORKING 4: 1400–1500

THE BEST YEARS?

After the Black Death there were far fewer people but landowners still needed workers for their land. Therefore landowners had to pay higher wages to stop their workers leaving the village. There was also plenty of land available and many peasants bought it at cheap prices.

These changes happened slowly but by the fifteenth century many ordinary people were richer and had more freedom than ever before.

What changed during this 'Golden Age'?

Source A

The English are rich, abounding in gold and silver and all the necessaries of life. They eat every kind of meat and fish. They are clothed with good woollens. They have abundant bedding and are rich in all household goods and agricultural equipment, and in all that is necessary for a quiet and happy life.

(Sir John Fortescue, an English Judge, writing in the 1460s)

Source B

The riches of England are greater than those of any other country in Europe, as I have been told by the oldest and most experienced merchants, and as I saw myself. There is no small innkeeper who does not set his table with silver dishes and drinking cups. There is an abundance of ale and beer and the people drink it in preference to wine. They all wear very fine clothes.

(Letter from a Venetian ambassador to England, 1497.)

WAS THERE CHANGE OR CONTINUITY IN	What kind of developments took place?	Why did they happen?	Who benefited the most? the landowners or the peasants?
Living conditions (pages 50–1)			
Opportunities for women (pages 52–3)			
Education and language (pages 54–5)			
Health and disease (page 56)			
Towns and trade (page 57)			

Source C

I sent your son to Lady Morley to find out what entertainment will be put on in her house at Christmas after the death of her husband. She said that there were no disguisings or harping or lute-playing or singing and no noisy amusements but there would be backgammon and chess and cards.

(From a letter written by Margaret Paston to her husband, John in 1459)

Source D

Wealthy merchants could afford to build houses like this in the towns, particularly in the sheep farming areas. Windows were glazed, chimneys were added and furniture included tapestries.

EVIDENCE: A GOLDEN AGE?

1. How do Sources **A**, **B** and **C** describe England in the fifteenth century?
2. Do you think that these writers are reliable witnesses? Explain your answer.
3. Which source do you think gives the most useful evidence?
4. You are going to investigate everyday life in the fifteenth century. What kinds of sources do you expect to use?
5. Copy the grid above. As you work through this chapter fill in the empty columns. This will tell you whether this was a 'Golden Age'.

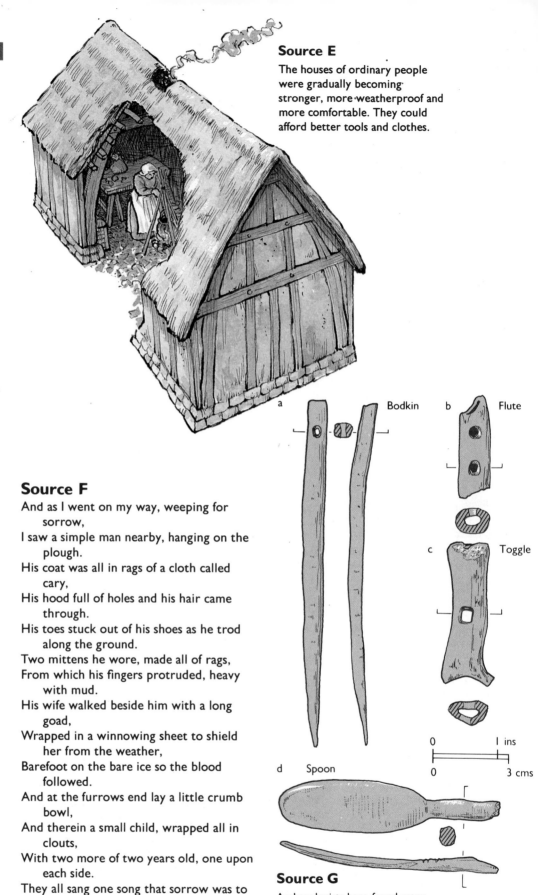

Source E

The houses of ordinary people were gradually becoming stronger, more weatherproof and more comfortable. They could afford better tools and clothes.

a   Bodkin   b   Flute

c   Toggle

0   1 ins

0   3 cms

d   Spoon

Source F

And as I went on my way, weeping for
    sorrow,
I saw a simple man nearby, hanging on the
    plough.
His coat was all in rags of a cloth called
    cary,
His hood full of holes and his hair came
    through.
His toes stuck out of his shoes as he trod
    along the ground.
Two mittens he wore, made all of rags,
From which his fingers protruded, heavy
    with mud.
His wife walked beside him with a long
    goad,
Wrapped in a winnowing sheet to shield
    her from the weather,
Barefoot on the bare ice so the blood
    followed.
And at the furrows end lay a little crumb
    bowl,
And therein a small child, wrapped all in
    clouts,
With two more of two years old, one upon
    each side.
They all sang one song that sorrow was to
    bear.
They all cried one cry, a miserable note
The simple man sighed sore and said,
'Children, be still.'

(From 'Piers the Ploughman' by William
Langland, written in the late 1300s)

Source G

Archaeologists have found many articles made from animal bones in medieval villages. These finds from Wharram Percy a village in Yorkshire were made from sheep and cattle bones.

Source H

Harvest workers' diet

Foodstuffs analysed by value

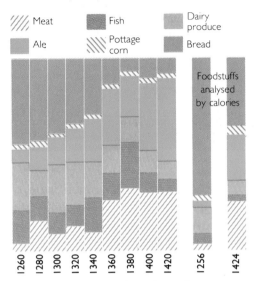

Meat • Fish • Dairy produce • Ale • Pottage corn • Bread

Foodstuffs analysed by calories

Here you can see how diets changed after the Black Death in the village of Sedgeford in Norfolk.

Source J

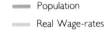

Population

Real Wage-rates

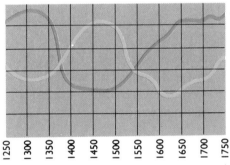

The graph shows when wages bought the most goods. Could people afford more before or after the Black Death?

Source I

The common people have become very proud. A wretched knave, working with a plough and cart, used to do well with a white shirt and a red gown. Now he must have a new doublet, worth at least 5 shillings and also a costly gown with fancy trimmings and a hood and colourful hose as though he were a squire. This pride is paid for by their masters who pay out the wages. Those who used to work for 10 to 12 shillings a year now demand 20 or 30 and do no more work.

(A priest's sermon written in the fifteenth century)

Net Annual Income

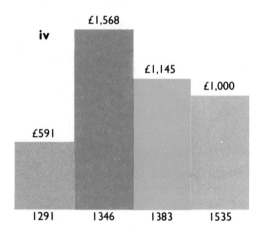

iv £1,568

£1,145

£1,000

£591

1291   1346   1383   1535

i   The daily pay of carpenters on the estates of the Bishop of Winchester.
ii The cost of renting an acre of land on the Bigod manor in Norfolk.
iii The price of a quarter of wheat on the estates of the Bishop of Winchester.
iv The money received from rents and sales of crops from his estates by the Abbot of Battle Abbey in Sussex.

Source K

Each lord kept detailed accounts for his land. The details in these accounts give historians a wealth of evidence.

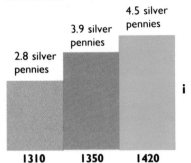

2.8 silver pennies   3.9 silver pennies   4.5 silver pennies

1310   1350   1420   i

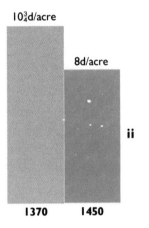

10¾d/acre   8d/acre

1370   1450   ii

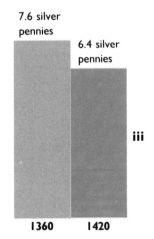

7.6 silver pennies   6.4 silver pennies

1360   1420   iii

EVIDENCE: WAS LIFE MORE COMFORTABLE?

1   Sources **D** to **K** tell us about the way people lived in the fifteenth century. Do the sources support the writers of Sources **A**, **B** and **C** on page 49?
2   Which sources are most useful for this investigation. Explain your answer.
3   Look at the pictures of the two houses (Sources **D** and **E**), both from the fifteenth century. Which household do you think left most evidence of their lives? Explain your answer.
4   Which of the two households improved the quality of their lives most during the fifteenth century?

◈ A golden age for women?

On these two pages you can see examples of the different kinds of jobs medieval women did:
A Nursing **B** Nuns **C** Spinning
D Farm work **E** Masons

Throughout the Middle Ages men and women shared work, except that women probably did more. They took care of children and made food but they also worked in the fields if they were peasants. If they were landowners they organized the castle and lands and dealt with lawyers because their lords were often away.

Therefore, many women had to do 'men's work', but they took second place when their husbands returned. After 1348 women had more chances to be independent because they could fill the gaps created by the Black Death. Some of the clearest evidence comes from London. Married and unmarried women were running their own businesses, trading and employing others. Some women became apprentices and joined guilds.

In Sheffield two women were blacksmiths. Others were named as the heads of households in Poll Tax records and many women were employed in the wool and cloth industries. In general women had more choice and control over their lives. As a result they did not marry until they were a little older and did not have so many children.

However, ideas about the place of women had not really changed. The influence of the Bible, saying that men were superior, was still strong. Therefore, when the population began to grow again there were fewer chances for women. By 1500 there were no women apprentices.

Education for girls

Although women had more opportunities, their education probably did not change.

Girls were mostly educated by their mothers. They were taught everything from making bread, butter and cheese to keeping accounts, dealing with lawyers and officials and preparing medicines, depending on how rich they were. The daughters of wealthy families were often sent to live in another house to learn dancing, music, needlework and even archery and riding.

Many girls, especially in wealthy families, did not choose their husbands. They married a

My own lady and indeed my true wife before God, I commend myself to you with a very sad heart as a man who cannot be cheerful and will not be until things change. We who ought to be most together are most apart. I realise lady that you have had as much sorrow on my account as any gentlewoman has had in this world. I wish to God that all the sorrow you have had had fallen on me so that you were freed of it. Indeed, lady, it kills me to hear that you are being treated other than you should be.

That was an extract from the only surviving letter between Richard and Margery. The rest were probably intercepted. Richard and Margery did marry but the Pastons did not forgive them easily. There must have been forgiveness in the end for Margery's mother, Margaret, left £20 to her grandson, John Calle.

man chosen by their parents. Sometimes the marriage was happy. Sometimes a girl rebelled.

Elizabeth Paston, was a trouble to her parents. When she was about 20, a neighbour wrote to Elizabeth's brother about the plan to marry Elizabeth to Stephen Scrope:

'If you can find Elizabeth a better husband I would advise you to do so quickly, because she was never in such sorrow as she is nowadays. She is not allowed to speak to anyone unless she deceives her mother. Since Easter she has usually been beaten once or twice a day, and sometimes thrice and her head has been cut in two or three places.

Elizabeth Paston did avoid marrying Stephen Scrope and rejected other proposals before she finally married when she was almost thirty. However even more marriage problems were to come for the Pastons. Girls were expected to marry richer husbands. Instead, Margery Paston fell in love with Richard Calle, the family's bailiff. Margery's brothers did not approve of her plans. One of them wrote about Richard Calle's 'plots' and then said 'even if my father and mother consented, he would never have my goodwill to make my sister sell candles and mustard in Framlingham.' However, their words made no difference.

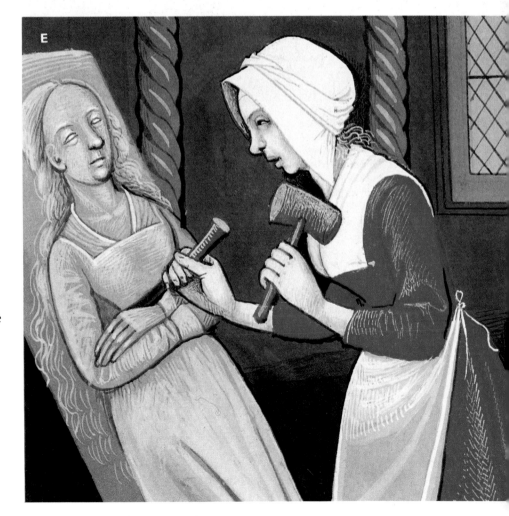

✦ Education, Language and Printing

Many families like the Pastons sent letters to friends and relatives all over the country. This tells us that many people were literate — perhaps 30 per cent of the population could read. Probably more could read in the large towns. The development of literacy and education was one of the most important changes in the fifteenth century and, in turn it led to the most important invention in the Middle Ages — printing. Why did these changes happen?

Women were often more literate than men. This picture shows a **woman teacher**

A page from one of the earliest books printed in England, by William Caxton. Caxton was born in Kent in 1422 but became rich as a merchant in Holland. He began printing there but returned to England in 1476. He wrote or translated books himself as well as printing them. He printed religious books, histories of King Arthur and the siege of Troy, Chaucer's Canterbury Tales and books on chess, hunting and manners.

More money, more books, more schools

Many people had more money. They used their money to send their children to school. Children no longer had to do the same jobs as their parents but they needed to be able to read and write before they could succeed. William Paston left detailed instructions in his will about his sons' education.

Many new schools were in towns. In grammar schools the sons of merchants and gentlemen learned Latin grammar. Monasteries also had schools for the sons of townspeople or wealthy villagers. Some of the children at monastic schools became monks. Others used their reading and writing skills in the family business. After school some boys went to university at Oxford or Cambridge. Many of them studied law which helped them to run their own lands. Others hoped to find work with the king's government or one of the great lords.

Printing

More people could read and write. They wanted books but by the middle of the fifteenth century the scriveners (copiers) could not copy books fast enough to meet the demand. A new way of making books quickly was needed and the answer was printing. William Caxton brought printing to England from Europe in the 1470's and printing began to affect the way people spoke English.

The importance of English

The chart below shows that English became more important than Latin and French in the fifteenth century. One important reason for this change was the war between England and France. Great victories like Agincourt in 1415 made English kings and people want to be English. It would have been strange if the king and nobles had kept on speaking French.

Although English was used by everyone each region of the country spoke its own kind of English. People from different regions had difficulty understanding each other. However one kind of English — or dialect — gradually became the most widely used. This was Midland English. You can see below some of the reasons why the Midlands dialect dominated the other local versions of English. Which do you think was the most important reason?

- Most of the population of England lived in the Midland area.
- Most people in London, Oxford and Cambridge spoke Midland English.
- The most famous writer of the time, Geoffrey Chaucer, wrote in Midland English.
- The first person to print books in England, William Caxton, printed books using Midland English. He began printing in 1476.

Midland English. Can you understand the poem below?

The Blacksmiths

Swart smeked smithes smatered with smoke
Drive me to deth with din of here dintes.
Swich nois on nightes ne herd men never:
What knavene cry and clatering of knockes.

(An anonymous 15th century poem)

Geoffrey Chaucer

Chaucer was born around 1342. His parents were well-off and he became a soldier and then a government official. He travelled a good deal and wrote many poems.

The most famous is The Canterbury Tales – a series of stories told by a group of pilgrims travelling to Canterbury. The stories, and Chaucer's descriptions of the pilgrims, tell us a lot about the people of the time. This picture shows him reading his stories to a group of lords and ladies.

How English became more important

	The King and nobles spoke	Government documents were written in	Ordinary people spoke
1350	FRENCH	LATIN and FRENCH	ENGLISH
1410	ENGLISH	LATIN and ENGLISH	ENGLISH
1460	ENGLISH	ENGLISH and LATIN	ENGLISH

◈ Health and Disease

Nobody in the middle ages, doctors included, really knew why people became ill. Many of the cures such as bloodletting and cauterising, often did not help the patient. Even so doctors charged high fees, so only the rich could afford them. Peasants relied on the village 'wise women' to cure their illnesses. Often the cure was made up from local herbs. Many of these herbal remedies did actually work.

Look at the sources on this page. Do you think that better diets and better hygiene were more important than doctors in keeping people healthy? You can check on diets by looking back to Source H on page 51.

People today often think that people in the Middle Ages were filthy and did not try to keep clean. Do you think medieval people were really like that?

Source M

For God's sake beware what medicines you take of any physicians of London. I shall never trust them because of your father and my uncle.

(Margaret Paston writing to her husband in 1464)

Source N

The evidence from excavations of peasant houses of the fourteenth and fifteenth centuries shows that:

- the houses usually had doorsills made of stone or wood
- the area around the doorway was usually reinforced with stones on the floor
- there are usually no layers of rubbish and other deposits on the floors
- drainage ditches were often dug around the house
- stone paths were built to the doors of some houses
- some house floors had a slight hollow to them from frequent sweeping.

Source O

The streets and lanes shall be cleansed of all impediment from dung. All streets and lanes leading towards the Thames from the King's highways, shall be kept clean. Each person shall make clean of filth the front of his house, under penalty of one mark. The Scavagers shall have the power to survey the street and remove all filth.

(The White Book of the City of London, 1419.)

Source P

The following are signs of death: continuous vomiting, a cold sweat, convulsions and delirium. If a blister, black in colour, appears upon his belly, the patient will die the following day; similarly if the face be distorted with swelling, the eyes become greenish, or the legs swollen.

Take the herb Cinquefoil and whilst collecting it say a Paternoster on behalf of the patient, and then boil it in a new jar and if the water be red in colour after this boiling, then the patient will die.

(From a set of instruction for doctors written around 1400)

Source Q

I say that the plague sores are contagious because they poison and corrupt the air. So it is best to flee from infected persons. In time of plague people should not crowd together because some may be infected. All four stinks are to be avoided – the stable, stinking fields, ways or streets, dead carrion and most of (all) STINKING WATERS. Keep your house so that infected air may not enter it. Let your house be clean and make a clear fire of flaming wood. Fumigate it with herbs

(From *A passing gde lityll boke necessarye agenst the Pestilence* first published in London in 1485)

Trade, markets and fairs

When people had more money they spent it at markets and fairs. At least once a week each town held a market. Local villagers sold eggs, butter, cheese and animals. Craftsmen sold household goods, such as pots and pans, shoes and needles.

Some towns also had the right to hold a fair once or twice a year. A fair was a mixture of entertainment and business. Silks, jewellery, weapons, spices and furs were sold while jugglers and acrobats performed. There was plenty of cheap ale and people watched animals fighting or the religious plays (called Mystery plays) paid for by the Guilds. Fairs were good for the local traders as people came from far away to spend their money. Towns that held fairs tried to stop other towns nearby gaining the right to hold a fair of their own.

There was plenty of cloth and wool at fairs because they were the most important parts of England's trade at home and abroad. At first England exported raw wool, the best in Europe. Most of the wool went to the Netherlands where it was turned into good quality cloth. English merchants would then buy back the finished cloth to sell in this country.

By the fifteenth century this trade had altered. English merchants were using the wool themselves to make good quality cloth. Places like Stamford and Norwich became centres for cloth making. Cloth was exported instead of wool.

The wool and cloth trades made many people wealthy. As more cloth was made merchants employed more people to weave and dye the cloth. Peasants in the villages could add to their incomes by spinning and weaving wool at home. Some of the houses built by rich cloth merchants in the fifteenth century are still standing.

A trading nation

England traded with the following countries; France, Spain, Italy, Russia, Greece, Germany, Norway, Sweden, India.
Which goods came from which countries?

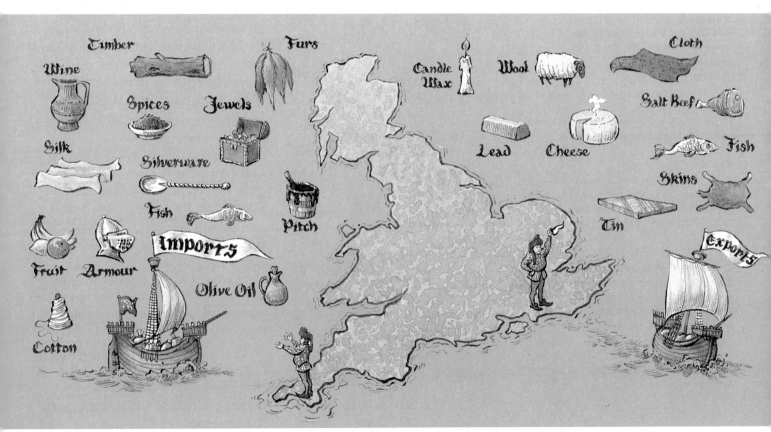

THE REVOLT OF 1381

What happened in 1381?

A

On 7 June the rebels in Kent freed John Ball, a priest, from Maidstone jail. Wat Tyler became their leader.

B

King Richard met the rebels at Mile End. Tyler demanded that all villeins should become freemen. The King agreed and pardoned the rebels.

C

The revolt began when villagers in Essex refused to pay taxes and attacked the tax collectors.

D

On the same day the king went by barge to meet the rebels on the banks of the Thames at Rotherhithe. Confusion amongst the rebels stopped him landing.

E

The rebels decided to march on London.

F

The King had another meeting with the rebels. Tyler made new demands but was stabbed by one of the king's men. The King ordered the rebels to disband and the revolt was over.

G

In the next few days the riots spread through Kent and Essex.

H

The rebels entered London and destroyed The Duke of Lancaster's palace. They freed prisoners and rioted. The King went into hiding.

I

Some rebels left London after being pardoned but others attacked the Tower of London and murdered two of the king's advisers.

J

The rebels assembled outside London.

Richard II goes to meet the rebels at Rotherhithe

Timeline

29	30	31	1	2	3	4	5	6	7	8	9	10	11	12	13	14	15	16

May   June

Scarborough
York
Beverley

Leicester
Northampton
Worcester
Dunstable
Berkhampstead
Bridgwater
Ilchester   Salisbury   Winchester

● Main centres of revolt
☐ Main counties in revolt

The changes you have been reading about did not all happen peacefully. After the Black Death peasants wanted more freedom and more pay but landowners opposed these changes. In many villages there must have been arguments but in 1381 the arguments turned into a revolt. Riots spread. Thousands of people marched on London. King Richard II, who was only fourteen, lost control of London to the rebels. This revolt was one of the most dramatic and frightening events of the Middle Ages.

Later in this chapter you can investigate who was involved in the revolt and why it happened, but first, try to work out from the clues on the left what happened during the Revolt of 1381. Draw a timeline of your own. Can you match the events to the bullets on the timeline?

⑤ Who was involved in the Revolt in 1381?

One of the puzzles about the revolt of 1381 is that people give it different names. Some historians called it the 'Peasant's Revolt'. Others have called it the 'Revolt of 1381' or the 'Great Revolt'. They disagree because it is difficult to decide who was involved in the revolt. Were only peasants involved?

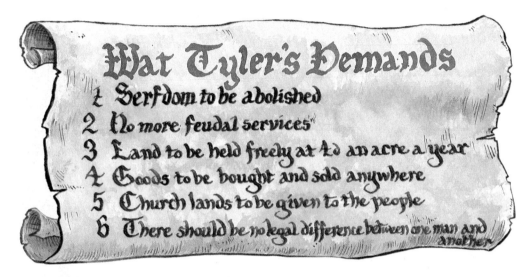

War Tyler's Demands
1 Serfdom to be abolished
2 No more feudal services
3 Land to be held freely at 4d an acre a year
4 Goods to be bought and sold anywhere
5 Church lands to be given to the people
6 There should be no legal difference between one man and another

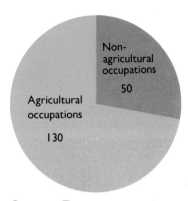

Source E
The Occupations of The Rebels
Taken from a sample of 180 rebels on the escheator's lists.

Source A

At about this time the Kingdom of England suffered a great and unexpected calamity. For the rustics, who we call serfs, together with other country dwellers living in Essex sought to better themselves by force.

(Thomas Walsingham, *A Chronicle of England*, 1380)

Source B

The frenzied mob trod upon the dead bodies. The peasant himself gave orders for life or death. The madman thirsted for blood more than a fish for water. If you sought mercy and wept like the waves of the sea for it, the tears would have no influence. When prayers were used, the peasant raged even more violently.

(John Gower, *The Voice of One Crying*, 1381. John Gower lived in London and was a landowner and poet. He started to write this description of the revolt in June 1381.)

Source C

Thomas Sampson, a Suffolk rebel, had 137 acres of crops, 300 sheep, 100 head of stock, an eight share in a ship.
William Gilebourne, a rebel from Fobbing, had 72 sheep and about 100 acres of land.

(Extracts from the Escheator's Lists of 1381. These records list land that was taken from the rebels.)

Source D

A complaint has been made in Parliament that many disturbers of the peace from Beverley, forgetful of its prosperity, have recently rebelled. They went up to the houses of several of our loyal subjects in armed force and threatened to kill them and throw down and burn their dwellings.

(From the records of Parliament in 1381)

Source F
The king talking to the rebels

DIFFERENT VIEWS: THE PEASANTS' REVOLT

1 Use only Sources A and B. Who was involved in the Revolt?
2 Use only Sources C and E. Who was involved in the Revolt?
3 How useful are Sources D and F for investigating who the rebels were? Explain your answer.
4 Why do you think some historians do not use the name 'the Peasants' Revolt'?
5 What do you think is the best name for the revolt?

⑤ How did Wat Tyler die?

The chroniclers of the 14th century wrote vivid accounts of the Revolt of 1381 but, as we have seen, there is plenty for historians to puzzle over. Several chronicles described the death of Wat Tyler, the rebels' leader. Can you work out what happened that day over 600 years ago?

The death of Wat Tyler

Source G

At Smithfield the King was approached by Tyler who stayed close to the King and drew his knife and kept throwing it from hand to hand. Tyler spoke threateningly, seizing the bridle of the King's horse. When the Mayor of London saw this he feared that the King would be killed and he knocked Tyler into the gutter. Thereupon, another squire, called Ralph Standish, pierced his side. And so he fell on his back and perished.

(Written by an anonymous author, probably a monk, at St. Mary's Abbey, Leicester. He was continuing Henry Knighton's *Chronicle of England* and wrote before 1395)

Source H

At Smithfield John Newton, a knight, came up to Wat Tyler on a war horse to hear what he proposed to say. Tyler became annoyed because the knight had approached him on horseback and not on foot. Newton said, 'As you are sitting on a horse it is not insulting for me to approach you on a horse.' At this Wat threatened to stab the knight and called him a traitor. The knight called Wat a liar and drew his knife too.

The King ordered Newton to descend from his horse and hand over his knife. But Tyler still tried to attack the knight so the Mayor of London and many royal knights and squires came to aid the King. Then the King, although of tender age, took courage and ordered the Mayor to arrest Tyler. The Mayor arrested Tyler and struck him a blow on the head. Tyler was soon surrounded by the other servants of the King and was pierced by sword thrusts in several parts of the body.

(From the chronicle of Thomas Walsingham – a monk at St Albans who wrote a chronicle of events in England between 1328 and 1388. he began his work in 1380. The monks at St Albans had many important visitors who provided information)

Source I

Wat Tyler sent for a jug of water because of the heat. As soon as the water was brought he rinsed out his mouth in a very rude manner in front of the King. As he did this a valet in the King's party said aloud that Tyler was the greatest thief in Kent. Wat would have killed the valet with his dagger in front of the King if the Mayor of London had not tried to arrest him. Wat angrily stabbed the Mayor, but the Mayor was wearing armour and was not harmed. He struck back at Wat, giving him a blow on the head. During this scuffle a valet of the King's household drew his sword and stabbed Wat two or three times, mortally wounding him.

(From *The Anonimalle Chronicle*, written by an unknown author who recorded the events of 1381 in great detail. He was most likely an eye-witness to the revolt and very probably a member of the King's party.)

EVIDENCE: THE DEATH OF WAT TYLER

1 How do the accounts in Sources **G**, **H** and **I** differ?
2 Why might the writers disagree?
3 In what ways do any of the accounts agree?
4 Why might the writers agree on some things?
5 Which account do you think is the most reliable?
6 Write your own account of Tyler's death, using only 80 words.

Why did the Revolt happen?

Historians need to do more than describe what happened. They also explain why things happened. It would be easy to say that the Revolt was caused by the effects of the Black Death but events usually have more than one cause. The diagram below shows a number of causes of the Revolt. Which of them were the most important?

The causes of the revolt

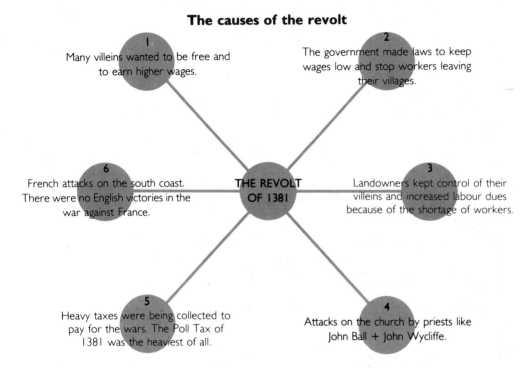

1 Many villeins wanted to be free and to earn higher wages.

2 The government made laws to keep wages low and stop workers leaving their villages.

6 French attacks on the south coast. There were no English victories in the war against France.

THE REVOLT OF 1381

3 Landowners kept control of their villeins and increased labour dues because of the shortage of workers.

5 Heavy taxes were being collected to pay for the wars. The Poll Tax of 1381 was the heaviest of all.

4 Attacks on the church by priests like John Ball + John Wycliffe.

Cause 1

'The labourers that have no land and work with their hands will no longer dine on the stale vegetables of yesterday. Penny ale will not suit them, nor bacon. They want fresh meat or fish, fried or baked. Unless he is highly paid he will bewail the time he was made a workman. Then he curses the King and all the King's justices for making such laws that grieve the labourer.'

(William Langland, *Piers Ploughman*, written in the late 1300s)

Cause 2

'Villeins who are idle and not willing to work after the pestilence without very high wages shall be ordered to work, in the place where they ought to work, receiving the usual salary and wages. Villeins refusing to serve in this way should be punished by imprisonment.

Each and every man and woman in our realm, free or unfree, who is strong in body and under sixty years of age, shall be bound to serve anyone who requires their services – unless they are living by trade, have property to live from or land to cultivate or are already in the service of others.'

(The Statute of Labourers of 1351. This law was introduced by the government to make sure that landowners had enough labourers at the lowest possible wage. Because there were fewer people workers hoped to get higher wages and do less work.)

CAUSES AND CONSEQUENCES: WHY DID THE REVOLT HAPPEN?

1 Which of the causes shown in the diagram were linked to The Black Death?
2 Which of the causes in the diagram were linked to war?
3 Which do you think was the most important cause of the Revolt?

Cause 3

The Court Roll for each manor was a sign that the peasants were not free. It recorded the taxes that the peasants had to pay to their lord and the work that they had to do for him. He could still control marriages, demand that villagers use his mill and ask for the best animal of the household when a tenant died. Even though many peasants earned higher wages and had more land they were still tied to their lord.

Cause 4

One of the leaders of the rebels was a priest called John Ball. Ball had been preaching for many years that all men were equal, even nobles and peasants. He also said that peasants should not pay the tithe to their village priest. Ball was imprisoned several times for his outspoken preaching but was released from Maidstone gaol by the rebels. In July 1381 he was executed by the government for taking part in the revolt.

Cause 5

The wars against France were going badly but the government taxed the people more and more to pay for armies. In 1377 the first Poll Tax was introduced. Everybody aged 15 years or older had to pay four pence in tax. There was another Poll Tax in 1379 and a third in 1381 when the tax had risen to one shilling per person. People had to pay the same whether they were landowners or poor peasants. For many people the Poll Tax of 1381 was the last straw.

Cause 6

'The French landed on the Isle of Wight in 1377. When they had looted and set fire to many places they then sailed along the English coastline burning many places and killing all the people they could find. In the same year the French assaulted the town of Winchelsea and sent a group of ships to burn the town of Hastings. They also invaded England close to Lewes in Sussex.

(Chronicle of Evesham Abbey, 1352–1392.)

Unlike today, people did not pay taxes every year. However, between 1371 and 1381 the government collected many taxes, which seemed even harder after twelve years without any taxes at all. A subsidy was a kind of tax.

The Burden of Taxation 1371–1381

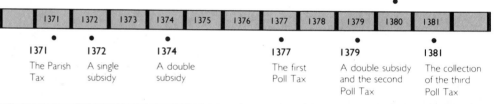

1371	1372	1374	1377	1379	1381
The Parish Tax	A single subsidy	A double subsidy	The first Poll Tax	A double subsidy and the second Poll Tax	The collection of the third Poll Tax

1380 — A subsidy and a half

The Black Death 1348	The Great Revolt 1381	The Fifteenth Century – A Golden Age?
This resulted in new choices for peasants: ● higher wages ● more land ● more freedom **But** ● landowners tried to stop or slow down these changes	This ended the Poll Taxes and also frightened the landowners so that they did not try so hard to stop change.	Ordinary people had higher wages, more land and more freedom. There were new chances for their children through education. **But** ● some towns suffered because there was less trade ● landowners made less profit **And** ● some important things did not change – farming methods and the dangers of disease

SUMMARY
Changes in everyday life 1300–1500

1   Do you think that the Black Death or the Great Revolt had a greater effect on people's lives?

2   Was the fifteenth century the best time to live in, between 1066 and 1500? Explain the reasons for your answer.

3   Between 1300 and 1500, do you think there was:
   a a lot of change in everyday life?
   b some change in everyday life?
   c hardly any change in everyday life?
   Give reasons for your answer.

ENGLAND AT WAR 2: 1300–1500

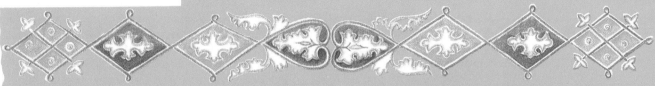

≣ An English archer

'Prepare your ground. Make ready.' The order forced John awake. He had been dozing, with his head resting on a bundle of arrows, dreaming of being back in England. He had been in France since early July. Now it was coming towards the end of August. He was ready to go home. Back in his village the harvest would be in. Celebrations would be underway.

As John dug his sharpened stake into the ground he thought of the early days of the campaign: the marching, the fighting and the looting. He had enough money to last him a while once he was home. He hoped they would all make it back to the ships.

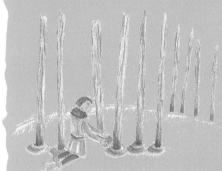

John packed the earth tight around the bottom of the stake with the heel of his boot. All the archers had prepared a line of stakes to hold back the French knights — if they got this far. In front of the stakes archers were still at work digging small holes to trap and break the legs of charging horses. John felt confident. King Edward had picked a good spot to bring the French to battle. The English army had the advantage of being on high ground. From their positions they could look down the wide valley along which the French army must come.

John lifted his head and looked at the throng of men on the hillside. Banners blew in the breeze, armour shone in the sun, the sound of last minute sharpening of weapons could be heard. Everything was surprisingly orderly and quiet. Everybody knew their lives could depend on how well they prepared. Archers, knights and footsoldiers were being carefully organised by the King's Earls. The King's son, who was only fifteen years old, had been given command of one of the blocks of men.

John sat down and untied one of the large bundles of arrows stacked behind the archers. he stuck a dozen arrows behind his stake, exactly where he would reach for them in the thick of the battle. He would use the arrows in less than a minute, but it would give him a good start. John's bow lay at his side: the six feet length of ash was bent taut by the bow string. He could do no more. Let the French come, he was ready.

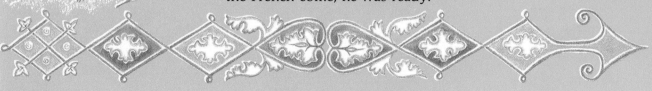

The sun was low in the sky when John first heard the sound of the French army. In the distance an endless stream of men seemed to be heading towards the English lines. They were well out of range. Strung across the front of the French forces and walking slowly was a line of crossbow-men, crossbows over their shoulders. They looked tired even from a distance. Behind the crossbow-men John could see the French knights. The English forces would be heavily outnumbered. Memories of John's village flashed through his mind again.

The English ranks were quiet. Like the other archers, John knew much depended on him. He brought an arrow to his bow ready for the command. He could see the crossbow-men more clearly now. The evening sun shining from behind him picked out their faces.
'Prepare to fire'. John lifted his bow high.
'Fire'. A hail of arrows descended on the crossbow-men.

John fired off his dozen arrows in the first minute and reached for more. He could see the enemy were already in confusion. The crossbow-men were still too far away for their bows to have any effect, so they did not fire. Some of them were retreating as arrows poured down on them. The French knights were trying to hack their way forward through their own crossbow-men. Then another hail of arrows stopped the knights in their tracks.

Horses fell in agony, knights collapsed as their armour was pierced. The French were in chaos, but still they poured into the valley, riding over their own dead and wounded. John did not need to aim. The ground in front of him was packed with the dead and dying and with knights urging their unwilling horses forward.

John continued to fire. In the heat of the battle he never considered why he was fighting: Perhaps later he would.

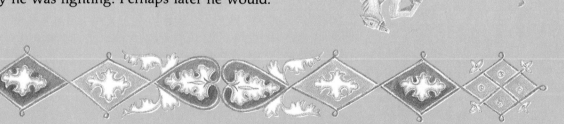

The Hundred Years War

In the first half of this book you discovered that war helped to change the way people lived in Britain. After 1300, war became an even more important cause of change because there were long periods of war when England fought France and Scotland.

What changes were caused by the wars?

The story you read on page 63 was about a battle that took place at Crecy in France. It was part of the 'Hundred Years War' which began in 1337. In 1346 Edward III won his first great victory, the Battle of Crecy, thanks to the skills of the archers. The war continued for well over a hundred years although there were long periods of peace. Eventually the French armies drove the English out of France.

Edward III claimed he was King of France and England

Edward held lands in France as a vassal of the French King. He therefore owed homage to Philip. Philip could call on Edward for service in time of war!

Philip VI, King of France, confiscated Aquitaine, an area of France under English control

Causes of the Hundred Years War

The French gave support to Scotland, a country England was fighting

Edward III was a king who enjoyed fighting and was good at it

Source A
Edward III paying homage to King Philip VI of France

Philip III
1270–1285

Philip IV
1285–1314

Charles of Valois

Louis of Evreux

Louis X
1314–16

Philip V
1316–22

Charles IV
1322–28

Isabella m Edward II
1307–27

Philip VI
1328–50

Edward III
1327–77

John II
1350–64

Charles V
1364–80

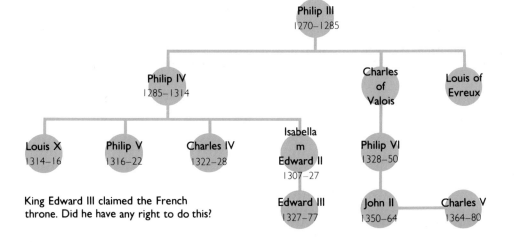

King Edward III claimed the French throne. Did he have any right to do this?

Source B
Edward III's claim to the French throne

CAUSES AND CONSEQUENCES: WHY DID THE WAR START?

1 Look at Source **B**. Why did Edward III think he should be King of France?
2 Look at Source **A**. Why did Edward object to this ceremony?
3 When Edward needed money he had to ask parliament for taxes. Which causes do you think he would have emphasised when he spoke to parliament? Give reasons for your answer.
4 What do you think were Edward's own motives for fighting the war?
5 Look back to the story. Were John's motives the same as the king's? Explain your answer.

☰ How did the war affect life in England?

The diagram below shows that the wars affected life in England a great deal. The questions and sources on these pages will help you work out whether the wars were popular and tell you some more about the effects of the wars.

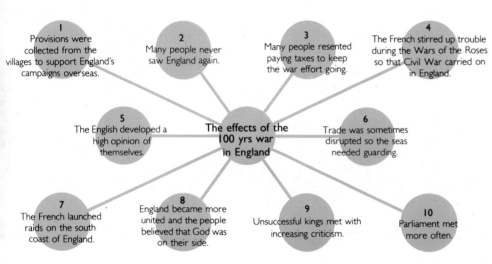

1 Provisions were collected from the villages to support England's campaigns overseas.

2 Many people never saw England again.

3 Many people resented paying taxes to keep the war effort going.

4 The French stirred up trouble during the Wars of the Roses so that Civil War carried on in England.

5 The English developed a high opinion of themselves.

The effects of the 100 yrs war in England

6 Trade was sometimes disrupted so the seas needed guarding.

7 The French launched raids on the south coast of England.

8 England became more united and the people believed that God was on their side.

9 Unsuccessful kings met with increasing criticism.

10 Parliament met more often.

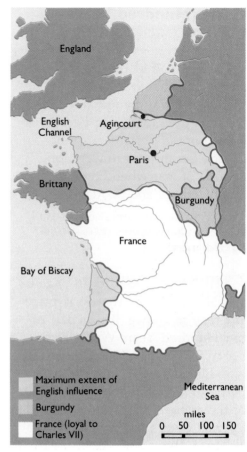

100 Yrs War territories

Source C

The effects of the Black Death on the English war effort.

Total Crown receipts of Edward III, including taxation.

1347 £142,588

1349 £101,281

Why do we see a fall in crown revenue?

Sacks of Wool Exported

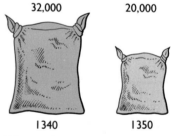

32,000 1340

20,000 1350

Why was less wool being exported?

Timeline : Hundred Years War

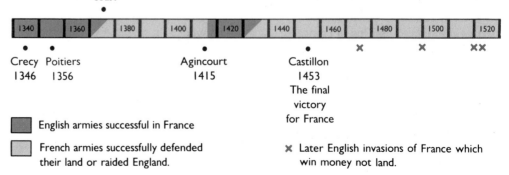

French raids on English coast

Crecy 1346

Poitiers 1356

Agincourt 1415

Castillon 1453 The final victory for France

☐ English armies successful in France

☐ French armies successfully defended their land or raided England.

✗ Later English invasions of France which win money not land.

Source D

Edward Montague agreed to serve in Brittany for 40 days with six knights, twenty men at arms, twelve men more lightly armed and twelve archers. For this he got wages of 76 pounds.

(An agreement made between the king and Edward Montague around 1340)

Source E

Our King went forth to Normandy
With grace and might of chivalry
There God for him worked marvellously
Wherefore England may call and cry
To God give thanks

May gracious God now save our king
His people and his well-willing
Give him good life and good ending
That we with mirth may safely sing
To God give thanks.

(From 'The Agincourt Carol' which celebrated Henry V's victory at the Battle of Agincourt in 1415.)

Source F

The King ordered his men to take from every county a fixed amount of quarters of corn, oats and bacon; every village according to whether it was large or small. Then from the Abbeys he took clothing, silver dishes and other ornaments to help his passage over the sea.

(Chronicle of Henry Knighton, 1338)

Source G

The French landed on the Isle of Wight on 21st August 1337. When they had looted and set fire to many places, they took a thousand marks as ransom for the Island. Then they returned to sea and sailed along the English coast. They burnt many places and killed, especially in the southern areas, all the people they could find.

(Chronicles of Nicholas Herford, Prior of Evesham Abbey, 1352–1392)

Source H

The Battle of Sluys, the only major naval battle of the Hundred Years War

Source I

Now the tax runs in England year after year, thus doing harm to all; by it those who were rich have come down in the world; and common folk must sell their cows, and even their clothing. The upkeep of those who are abroad is too costly; now there is not the wealth in their lands to maintain them.

(An anonymous poem, written about 1337–40)

Source J

Keep then the seas about in special;
Which of England is the round wall,
As though England were likened to a city
And the wall environ the sea.

(A political poem of the 1430s)

Source K

The English are great lovers of themselves. They think that there are no other men than themselves and no other world but England. Whenever they see a handsome foreigner they say 'he looks like an Englishman'. They do not like foreigners.

(A report by a Venetian ambassador in 1497)

Source L

The King of France is urging the Earl of Warwick to return to England. He has offered his ships and troops to fight against King Edward.

(A report from the Milanese ambassador in France, 1470)

THE EFFECTS OF THE WARS

1 Read Source **D**. Why did the kings need to raise taxes for the wars?
2 Look at the time-line and Source **C**. When do you think it was difficult for the king to raise taxes? Explain your answer.
3 Sources **E** to **L** are evidence of the effects of the wars. Can you match one source to each of the effects numbered **I** to **8** in the chart?
4 We will look at effects **9** and **10** more carefully in the next chapter. To help you start thinking about them, why do you think these were effects of the war?
5 Which of the effects in the chart do you think were the most important. Explain your answer.
6 Do you think that the war was popular? Explain your answer.

Britain – one medieval realm?

Powerful English kings, like Henry II, had always tried to control the rest of Britain. They did not have much success until Edward I conquered Wales in the 1280s. However, even Edward could not win control over Scotland and no English king had ever had much power in Ireland. During the Hundred Years War English kings were even keener to control the rest of Britain. These pages will help you find out whether they succeeded.

Source M

The King of France was striving by all means to harm the King of England. He helped and supported the Scots, the enemies of England, so that the Scottish war would delay England from attacking France.

(A statement by Edward III in 1337)

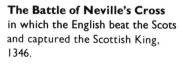

The Battle of Neville's Cross in which the English beat the Scots and captured the Scottish King, 1346.

BRITAIN: ONE REALM OR MANY?

1 Read Source **M**. Why was Scotland important to English kings?
2 What other evidence tells us that England wanted to control Scotland?
3 When was Wales most dangerous to England?
4 Why were there rebellions in Wales?
5 English kings could control Wales more easily than Ireland. Why?
6 France allied with Scotland but not with Ireland. Why?
7 Did the Hundred Years War cause more wars within Britain? Explain your answer.
8 Why did England fail to win control over the rest of Britain?
9 '*The tyranny and cruelty of the English are famous all over the world.*' This was written by a Scot in 1442.
   a Do you think that other Welsh, Scots and Irish shared his attitude to the English?
   b What might an Englishman have said in reply?

Why were Scotland, Ireland and Wales important to the English?

1334
Edward III defeats Scots. Scottish King flees to France

1402
Scots. defeated

1419
Scottish troops sent to help the French

1388
English defeated

1346
Scottish King captured at battle of Neville's Cross

The Kildare family control much of Ireland for England

The Pale

1404
Aided by the French Glyndwr captures Harlech

1490's
Support for pretenders to the English throne

1403
Henry IV defeats the Percys

Owain Glyndwr controls most of Wales and raids England

1405
French troops sent to help Owain Glyndwr

● Towns

■ Castles

Scotland, Bannockburn, Halidon Hill, Berwick, Homildon Hill, Otterburn, Newcastle, Neville's Cross, Ireland, Dublin, Conway, Rhuddlan, Caernarvon, Flint, Harlech, Shrewsbury, Aberystwyth, Buith, Wales, England, France

Scotland

Edward I failed to conquer Scotland and the Scots then hit back hard. They won the Battle of Bannockburn in 1314 and raided England. In 1328 Edward III agreed that Scotland was a separate kingdom. England could not conquer Scotland. It was too far away, war was expensive and the Scots were too determined. Fighting in the borders carried on, especially when England was at war with France. France and Scotland helped each other. In 1419 a Scottish army went to France to fight against England.

Owain Glyndwr

Glyndwr was the leader of the Welsh rising of the early 15th century. He was born in 1359 and went to study law in London. He was a large landowner who argued in 1401 with Lord Grey over the ownership of some land. Henry IV was reluctant to settle the dispute in his favour, so Glyndwr attacked and burnt Lord Grey's estates. The violence spread as Glyndwr promoted himself a leader of the Welsh nationalists against the English. He had followers throughout Wales, and successfully captured many English strongholds in Wales. By the summer of 1403 Glyndwr was attacking English estates in Herefordshire and Shropshire. He was helped by the French who signed an alliance with him in 1404. He fought from the mountains of Wales against the English forces until his death in 1416.

Ireland

English rulers never really tried to conquer Ireland completely. Ireland was not rich enough to provide much money and it did not threaten England because it was further away. However Ireland was not peaceful. The Irish fought the English settlers, and by 1400 the English only controlled a small area around Dublin called 'The Pale'. The rest of the country was controlled by native Irish lords. During the Hundred Years War, England ignored Ireland because it was not a threat. The English only became worried in the 1490s when rebels used Ireland as a base.

Wales

Wales had been conquered by Edward I. After 1300 there was only one serious rebellion, led by Owain Glyndwr in 1400. Glyndwr won control over most of Wales and then joined some English nobles in a civil war against Henry IV. If the rebels had won, Wales would have become a separate country. The English armies had difficulty fighting in the Welsh mountains and France sent help to Wales. Eventually English power, money and Henry V's military skill won.

THE POWER OF THE KING 2: 1300–1500

Richard II (1377–1399)

When Richard was 14 he bravely faced the Great Revolt. However this success did not continue. He chose his friends as advisers and ignored some of the most powerful nobles. When the French wars went badly the nobles tried to limit Richard's power. However they did not try to depose him.

Richard never forgave his opponents. In 1397 he had them murdered or exiled. One of the exiles was Henry, Duke of Lancaster. Henry had to choose between losing all his wealth or returning to attack Richard. He returned and forced Richard to abdicate. Henry became King Henry IV.

Henry V (1413–1422)

He was the son of Henry IV. As soon as Henry became king there were rebellions. However he crushed the rebels and then united the nobles for a war against France. He won a great victory against France at Agincourt in 1415 and then conquered more of France. He was very religious and he also made sure that the laws were obeyed. He was ruthless but people were loyal to him because they could trust him.

In Chapter 3 you discovered that the king's power increased after 1066. Sometimes this led to civil war because the barons complained that the king was not asking for their advice and was treating them harshly. In the reigns of John and Henry III the barons tried to control the king's power by making agreements with the king. However they could not force the king to keep agreements like Magna Carta. Kings said that they were chosen by God and could not be controlled by anyone else.

After 1300 there were more struggles between kings and their barons – or nobles as they were now called. This chapter investigates these struggles.

Were there any more changes in the king's power?

Timeline

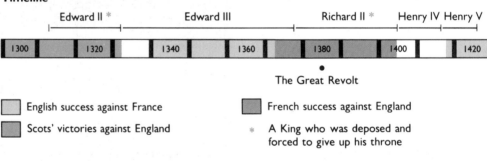

The Great Revolt

| | English success against France | | | French success against England |
| Scots' victories against England | | | * | A King who was deposed and forced to give up his throne |

WHY DID KINGS SUCCEED OR FAIL?

1 Look at the timeline and the information about Henry V. Why was he successful?
2 Look at the information about Richard II. He was deposed – forced to give up being king. Why was he unsuccessful?
3 Imagine that you have been asked to give advice to a new king. What three things would you say to him? Explain why you have chosen these three pieces of advice.
4 Do you think that nobles were keen to depose kings? Explain your answer.

Henry VI – would you have deposed him?

Two kings had been deposed and murdered, but a good king was just as important as ever. The nobles wanted a king – a good leader who they could trust. Nobody thought of doing without a king.

Henry V was the ideal king. He kept law and order, he was very religious and a great soldier – the nobles followed him willingly to war. When he died his son became king, aged nine months old! The nobles did not try to stop little Henry VI being king. They governed the country for him and trained him to be king but Henry was very different from his father. He was a very poor king.

By 1455 it looked as if Henry VI would lose his crown. Some nobles had rebelled and had beaten Henry's army at the Battle of St Albans. Their leader, Richard, Duke of York, met King Henry who was sheltering in St Albans abbey. The Duke of York was related to Henry and some said that he was the true king. What should York do? Should he:

- send Henry to prison and become king himself?
- allow Henry to stay as king and become his chief adviser?

Look at the rest of this page. What would you have advised York to do? What arguments would you use to back up your choice?

Henry VI

Henry VI's problems

- The French slowly won back the lands that Henry V and his armies had conquered.
- Henry VI did not do enough to stop people breaking the law. Nobody was afraid that Henry would punish them severely – in 1450 he fled when rebels attacked London.
- Henry VI had a small group of favourite advisers and he gave them lots of his own land so that he became poorer. Even so, hardly anyone criticised Henry himself. They always blamed his 'evil councillors'.
- Henry refused to choose his cousin, Richard, Duke of York, as one of his advisers. Instead he chose the Duke of Somerset who was York's enemy. York said that Somerset was a traitor for surrendering Rouen in France without fighting.
- When Henry VI had been ill for 18 months the nobles chose York to rule the country. Somerset was put in prison. He was freed as soon as Henry recovered but he was killed at St. Albans.

Richard, Duke of York

The Stages of the Wars of the Roses

1
1459–1461 (White Rose)
The Yorkists beat the Lancastrians. Although Richard, Duke of York was killed, his son became King Edward IV. Henry VI, Queen Margaret and their son had to escape abroad.

2
1469–1470 (Red Rose)
Edward's main adviser, the Earl of Warwick, rebelled because he wanted more power. He changed sides and joined the Lancastrians. He attacked Edward and forced him to escape abroad. Warwick made Henry VI king again.

3
1471 (White Rose)
Edward IV won the throne back. He killed Warwick and Henry VI and his son. Edward ruled England successfully until he died in 1483. His son became King Edward V, Aged 13 years old.

Lancaster against York

✠ The Wars of the Roses

'The Duke of York came to the king. On his knees he asked for the king's forgiveness, saying that he had never intended to hurt the king.'

So York did not become king. He had always been careful to say that he was only criticising the king's advisers, like the Duke of Somerset, not the king. The nobles still wanted Henry, even if he was not a good king, because he had been chosen by God.

Four years later the fighting started again. This was the beginning of the Wars of the Roses, when the family of Henry VI – the Lancastrians – fought the family of Richard of York – the Yorkists. There were many battles but most people's lives were not affected by the wars.

What do the wars tell us about the power of the king? People wanted a strong king. They were happy to have Edward IV as king because he was tall, handsome and generous. More importantly he was a good soldier and could keep law and order. England was much more peaceful after he had finally beaten the Lancastrians in 1471.

Even the nobles did not want the wars to continue. Many did their best to stay out of the fighting. Being on the losing side meant that your family lost its lands and riches. So the wars were kept going by just a few people. Look at the chart below that shows the situation in 1461.

Edward IV
He was only 18 when he became king. Suddenly he became the most powerful man in the country

Margaret and her son
They escaped abroad. Margaret wanted to win back the crown for her son

Richard, George and Warwick
When Edward became king they were given many rewards, including land and money. They thought Edward would be a much better king

Oxford and Somerset
They had lost all their lands and money. They also thought that Henry still should be king

WHY DID THEY FIGHT?

1 Why do you think the Lancastrians continued to fight after 1461?
2 The Lancastrians won the crown back in 1470 and Edward IV had to escape abroad. Why do you think he did not just give up and live quietly?
3 Do you think these people were just bloodthirsty or did they have good reasons for fighting? Explain your answer.

Richard III – the odd king out

In this chapter we have investigated some poor kings — kings who lost wars, could not keep law and order and did not listen to the advice of their nobles. In 1485 another king, Richard III, was deposed, but he was different. Richard III was a good soldier, he had kept law and order in the north when he was a Duke and he had been popular. He was also the brother of the popular Edward IV. What went wrong for Richard III?

The simple answer is that people believed that he had killed his two nephews (Edward IV's sons) so that he could become king. Many people rebelled against him but when the rebellion failed they escaped to France. There they found a new leader, Henry Tudor. After this Richard was always afraid of an invasion. In August 1485 Henry Tudor landed in Wales with an army of Englishmen, Welshmen and some Frenchmen.

As Henry Tudor marched into England, Richard sent messages all over the country, hoping that many men would join his army.

Richard III

- He was the brother of Edward IV and was always loyal to Edward.
- He was a good general who led armies against Scotland.
- In the north of England he was popular and kept law and order.
- His nephews disappeared and most people said he murdered them.
- Since becoming king he had given a lot of lands and other rewards in the south to his northern supporters.

Henry Tudor

- He was related to Henry VI so he had some royal blood.
- Nobody in England knew him because he had been in hiding in France.
- He had no training for being king and had never led an army in battle.
- Many Englishmen who used to support Edward IV now supported Henry because they believed Richard killed
- He had help from the King of France who was afraid that Richard might invade France.
- He had to be clever and cautious to escape capture while he was in living in France.

The Family of the Duke of York

```
                    Richard,        Cicely
                    Duke of York    Neville
         ┌──────────────────┼──────────────────┐
      EDWARD IV          George,            RICHARD III
   (king 1461–1483)   Duke of Clarence    (king 1483–1485)
                       (killed 1478)
   ┌────────┬──────────────────┐
Elizabeth           Princes in the
married    Edward V  Tower. They     Richard
Henry VII           disappeared in
c 1486               1483
```

TAKING SIDES

1 What would you have done when you got Richard's message? There are three choices:
   a Ride to join Richard and fight against Henry.
   b Ride to join Henry and fight against King Richard.
   c Wait to see what the result of the battle is and then support the winner.

2 What aspects of their own lives might have affected people's choice about fighting in 1485?

✠ 1485 – a turning point in history?

Many Englishmen did not support King Richard at the Battle of Bosworth. Even some who joined his army did not fight. Richard died bravely, charging on horseback against Henry Tudor who became Henry VII, the first Tudor king.

Henry VII when he was middle aged

For most of his reign Henry had to work hard to keep the crown. He was always afraid of rebellions or invasions but he did make the country more peaceful. One important reason was that the nobles were happy to co-operate with him. They had learned that rebellion was dangerous. The best way to keep their lands and riches was to obey the king.

✠ The importance of Parliament

One of the main political changes after 1300 was that there were many more parliaments. Kings had to ask parliament for taxes because of the wars with France or Scotland. Often the members of the Commons also took the chance to criticise the king's policies. However parliament did not really have much power. It could not change the king's policies. The king could close parliament whenever he wished and he did not need to have a parliament at all unless he needed taxes.

Look at the information on the timeline (below).

Timeline : Reign of Henry VII 1485–1509

• Years when there were rebellions or the king feared an invasion.

☐ Years when there was a parliament.

HOW MANY PARLIAMENTS?

1 How many parliaments met during Henry VII's reign?
2 Why were there fewer parliaments in the second half of Henry's reign?
3 Henry called only one parliament in the last 11 years of his reign. Do you think that parliaments might have stopped meeting for ever?

The power of the king 1066–1500

This page will help you to summarize the changes in the power of the king between 1066 and 1500. Use the information on this page as the basis of your answers. Information in the rest of the book will add to your answers.

1   A group of barons forced King John to agree to Magna Carta because he had been using his power unfairly against them. However Magna Carta was not a success. John broke the agreement.

2   Edward I was a strong king and started a long series of wars. He called parliament regularly to get taxes for his wars.

3   Henry II ruled the great Angevin Empire and gained more power for the king.

4   When Henry VII became king many nobles were tired of civil war. They were happy to co-operate with the king. Henry did not call parliament very often because he did not need money for wars abroad.

5   William the Conqueror won control over the whole country, land and people after the Battle of Hastings.

6   Edward II was deposed because the barons could not trust him to keep agreements. He had just a few favourite advisers instead of consulting all the barons.

7   Henry VI was a poor king but nobody wanted to depose him. People did not think he was wicked. He was only deposed after wars started between his advisers and their opponents.

8   Parliaments met for the first time in Henry III's reign. They were started as meetings of barons who wanted to control the king's actions. However Henry III broke the agreement and did not call parliaments.

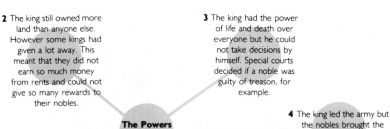

2 The king still owned more land than anyone else. However some kings had given a lot away. This meant that they did not earn so much money from rents and could not give so many rewards to their nobles.

3 The king had the power of life and death over everyone but he could not take decisions by himself. Special courts decided if a noble was guilty of treason, for example.

1 The king was God's representative so he was difficult to criticise but sometimes kings had been deposed.

The Powers of the King

4 The king led the army but the nobles brought the soldiers. The king did not have his own army.

7 The king needed to ask parliament for taxes for war. There were many wars after 1300. When parliament met it could criticise the king or accuse his advisers of treason.

6 The king needed the nobles to keep law and order in the country, especially further from London.

5 The king made all the decisions but the nobles expected him to ask for their advice. He could not just listen to a few, favourite advisers.

THE POWER OF THE KING 1066–1500

1   Copy the timeline and then add the 8 statements at the right places on the timeline. Use the information in the rest of the book to help you.

2   Which two kings had the most power? Give reasons for your answer.

3   When did the barons first try to limit the power of the king?

4   When did parliaments first meet?

5   Why did parliaments start to meet?

6   Why was the first king deposed?

7   Why did parliaments meet much more often after 1272?

8   How did the Wars of the Roses affect the power of the king?

9   Which of these two statements do you agree with? Explain the reasons for your answer.

a   The nobles usually wanted a strong king they could trust. They wanted to co-operate with the king.

b   The nobles were usually keen to attack or depose the king because they had more power if there were civil wars.

10   King John ignored Magna Carta. Why then do historians say that Magna Carta was so important?

11   Between 1066 and 1500 had the power of the king changed:

a   a lot?

b   a little?

Explain the reasons for your answer.

FINISHING YOUR INVESTIGATION

Source A

This picture is from a book owned by a French nobleman. It was made about 1416. Rich English people also had books like this, full of beautiful, colourful pictures. Many of the books were prayer books. Real life was just as full of colour in clothes and buildings.

Source B

A stained glass window showing Adam as a fifteenth century peasant. Churches were full of colourful windows and the walls were painted with scenes from the Bible. Delicate wooden carvings helped to make churches beautiful.

▥ A dark and dreary world?

In the Middle Ages people had no electricity, no gas and therefore no light bulbs, no central heating and no televisions. It is easy to feel sorry for them. However in the 11th century a visiting merchant wrote:

'All the riches and delights of the world are found in England. On all sides there are fruitful fields, milky herds and good warhorses. It is watered by bubbling streams and rivers, teeming with fish and fowl. The vineyards rival those of France. Shellfish provide shining pearls but even more beautiful is the gold cloth woven by English maidens. There are rich metals — copper, iron, lead, tin, silver and gold.'

At the end of the Middle Ages, visitors still marvelled at the riches of England. The lives of ordinary people had improved but just a few people — the king and his lords, the bishops and the abbots — still owned most of the wealth. What did they spend their money on? These pages give you some ideas but you can also use the rest of this book to answer the questions on the right.

Timeline : periods of prosperity

Black
Death

●

| 1000 | | | 1100 | | | 1200 | | 1300 | | | 1400 | | | 1500 |

▢ Improvements/greater wealth for most people.

▢ Hardship for many.

PEOPLE IN THE PAST: MEDIEVAL ENGLAND

Source C

Tattershall castle was built in the fifteenth century from brick, because it was more attractive than stone. The large windows let in as much light as possible. It looked like a castle but it was really meant to show off the owner's wealth and importance.

Source D

This gold candlestick made for Gloucester Cathedral shows how careful and delicate craftsmen could be. Their skills improved throughout the Middle Ages.

Use the sources on these pages and any others in this book to answer the following questions.

1 Do you think that:
   a medieval people were skilful?
   b medieval people lived comfortable lives?
   c medieval people were only interested in fighting?
   Explain the reasons for your answer.

2 Was life in the Middle Ages:
   a the same as life today?
   b different from life today?

3 Compare life in medieval England with another time you have studied. Was life in the two periods the same or different?

4 Religion was very important in the Middle Ages. How did religion affect:
   a art and architecture?
   b holidays and entertainments?
   c wars such as the Crusades?
   d attitudes to the king?

5 Art and architecture changed quite a lot during the Middle Ages. Why do you think they changed?

6 Look at the timeline. If you could go back to the Middle Ages which century would you live in? Explain your choice.

7 Do you think that life in the Middle Ages was dark, dreary and uncomfortable? Give reasons for your answer.

Clue A: The King and the government

In 1066 the King of England made all the decisions about how to run the country. He did not have to take advice from anyone but he depended on the lords to bring men for his army. The King of England did not control Scotland, Wales or Ireland. Sometimes English kings even had difficulty controlling the distant parts of England.

Clue B: The Priests and religion

In 1066 almost everyone went to church every week and on holy days. There was only one kind of Christianity, the Catholic Church, led by the Pope in Rome. Ordinary people had to pay taxes to their local priests and richer people gave gifts to the church.

Clue C: Everyday Life

In 1066 nearly everyone earned their living by farming in the countryside. Some people were so poor that they would starve to death if there were bad harvests but many were better off. However, even the richer peasants were not free. They had to work on their lord's land and could not leave their village without his permission. Work was hard because people and animals were the only kinds of energy.

Early printers at work.

When you began this book you saw the 3 clues on the left. They describe what life was like in 1066.

1   Rewrite these clues so that they describe life in 1500.
2   In the Middle Ages was there:
    a   a lot of change?
    b   some change?
    c   no change?
    Explain why you have chosen your answer.
3   Which parts of British life were most affected by:
    a   the Norman Conquest?.
    b   population and climatic change 1100–1300?
    c   the Black Death?
    d   civil and foreign wars?
4   Which of these causes do you think was the most important? Explain your answer.
5   One event in the 1470s was going to cause great changes.
    a   What was the event?
    b   Why do you think it would cause many changes?
6   Would you like to have lived during the Middle Ages? Explain your answer.

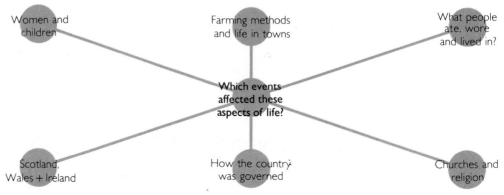

Life in 1500:

- In 1500 nearly everyone still lived by farming.
- In 1500 most people lived more comfortably than in 1066.
- Nearly everyone was free to live and work where they wished.
- Religion was still important.
- Many people could read and printing had been invented.
- People still wanted a strong and powerful king to defend the country and keep law and order.
- Parliaments were called to give the king taxes.
- Scotland was still independent but Wales had been conquered. English kings were starting to be more involved in Ireland.

▌▊▊ Historical skills and ideas

By now you will have checked your hypothesis and perhaps changed it. You have a good answer to the question that began the book. In this investigation you have been working like a historian and learning about the problems historians have. The questions below will help you sum up what you have learned.

EVIDENCE

1 List five sources of evidence about medieval Britain.
2 Do you always believe what sources tell you? Explain the reasons for your answer.
3 What questions would you ask to check whether a source is reliable?
4 'If a source is biased it is useless for a historian.' Do you agree with this?
5 'Historians should always agree because they have the same sources.' Explain why you agree or disagree with that statement.

The Bayeux Tapestry is a good source of evidence about the Norman Conquest

Yes, but remember it is biased and only tells the Norman side of the story

CAUSES AND CONSEQUENCES

When historians investigate causes and effects they do three things.

  i identify a number of causes or effects
 ii put them in order of importance
iii say what they're not certain about

1 Why might historians be uncertain about what caused an event?
2 Which of the three answers on the right do you think is the best?
3 Why might historians disagree about the causes or effects of an event?

There are three reasons why the barons quarelled with King John, war, taxes and his cruelty

I think that war was the most important cause of the quarrel between John and his barons

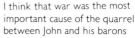

I think that high taxes was the most important cause of the quarrel between John and his barons but wars and his cruelty also worried the barons

CHANGE AND CONTINUITY

1 Look at Answers **1** and **2**. Why is Answer **2** better than Answer **1**?
2 Answer **3** is better than Answer **2**. What does this pupil understand about change and continuity that the pupil who gave Answer **2** doesn't?
3 Answer **4** is the best. Why?
4 Why might historians sometimes disagree about change and continuity in the Middle Ages?

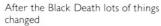

After the Black Death lots of things changed

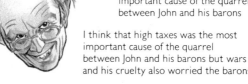

The Black Death caused many changes – ordinary people had higher wages, more freedom and more land

The Black Death changed many things but some things stayed the same

There was both change and continuity after the Black Death but there was probably more change. People at the time thought life was changing fast

INDEX

Oxford University Press,
Walton Street, Oxford OX2 6DP

Oxford New York Toronto
Delhi Bombay Calcutta Madras
Karachi Petaling Jaya Singapore
Hong Kong Tokyo Nairobi
Dar es Salaam Cape Town
Melbourne Auckland

and associated companies in
Berlin Ibadan

Oxford is a trademark of
Oxford University Press

Typeset by MS Filmsetting
Limited, Frome, Somerset
Printed in Italy.
by G. Canale & C. S.p.A.
Borgaro T.se - Torino

▥ Notes to teachers

Exercises offering opportunities for developing
pupils' understanding of the concepts and skills
required in Attainment Targets, are signposted
as follows. Most, but not all, of the questions in
these exercises are linked to Statements of
Attainment, as too encyclopaedic a coverage
would be an intolerable burden for everyone.

AT1a   Changes   11 17 19 40 46 62 79
AT1b   Causes and
          Consequences   19 40 61 65 79
AT1c   People in the Past   45 77
AT2   Different Views   21 24 59
AT3   Evidence   33 37 44 49 60 79

Last but not least, pages 41 and 79 provide the
opportunity to summarise the development of
pupils' understanding of how history is studied.
Explicit discussion of the stages involved in
analysing the value of sources or explaining why
an event happened is vital for enhancing pupils'
understandings.

Ian Dawson   Paul Watson